becoming
julie
my incredible journey

julie clarke

Published by Fledgling Press, 2014
Cover Design: Graeme Clarke
graeme@graemeclarke.co.uk

www.fledglingpress.co.uk

Printed and bound by:
Bell & Bain Ltd, Glasgow

ISBN: 9781905916832

Description of Gender Dysphoria from www.transwirral.btik.com

acknowledgements

Writing this book has been an amazing experience. Although, I had to revisit some very dark and painful memories along the way. However it has been an emotional but cathartic undertaking.

First and foremost I'd like to thank the handful of folk, who in the early years were brave enough to stand up and support and encourage me. At a time when society wasn't ready to accept those of us who didn't seem to conform to what was perceived to be normal, and took an alternative path in life. All of those people are the true heroes and heroines in this book, but I'd like to single out Sue, Sheila, Irene and Peter. Without them I probably wouldn't be here today.

I must commend Elaine Barrie for her courage, tolerance and support over many years. Also I'd like to thank Veronica for her support and for cheering me up when I was feeling vulnerable. A special thought goes out my dear departed friend Marcia who stuck by me through thick and thin.

To my special friends Ian and Terri, a heartfelt thanks for being there when I really needed support at a crucial time of my journey.

A special thanks to my GP, Dr. O'Neil, who was the first health professional to take me seriously, and was the one who started the ball rolling, which would make the necessary physical changes to my body, and she became enthusiastic about helping me through the final part of my transition. Without all of the people mentioned above, I doubt if I'd be the woman I am today.

However this book would not have been possible without the help and advice from those in the literary world. Thanks to Maggie McKernan for her advice and appraisal of my original manuscript. A big thanks to my editor Mandy Woods, who worked with me to bring the manuscript up to a standard, where I could confidently submit it to publishers. Last and most definitely not least, of course, a huge thanks to my publishers, Fledgling Press, who made this book happen. A special thanks to Clare, Graeme, Paul and everyone else involved in my book.

Everyone deserves a chance in life, but more often than not you will need others to help you realize your dreams. Thank you from the bottom of my heart to everyone who helped me realise mine.

Julie Clarke
Isle of Coll, September 2014

This Book Is Dedicated To:

Sue Clarke
Sheila Bidwell
Marcia Gratwick

Sue was the first person who believed in me, and was prepared to accept me for who I was, and what I aspired to be, she took me under her wing at a time when I believed there was nowhere for me to go. She quite literally sowed the seeds of my self-belief, which would eventually set me on my path to true womanhood.

Sheila came into my life at arguably the darkest days of my journey, at a time when I felt that only my demise would free me from my inner turmoil. She was the one who recognized the female within me. She gave me the courage to walk tall and hold my head up high, and to persevere with what I believed in, even through the groundswell of prejudice that had built up towards me.

Marcia was a solid rock, a selfless true friend by my side, just when I needed loyal support, she stuck with me come what may. She was prepared to take the flak alongside me, and stood shoulder to shoulder with me at a time, when I received fierce opposition and prejudice to the path I had taken.

My three dear friends are sadly no longer with us. However they were instrumental in shaping the confident woman I have become today, their memory will remain in my heart always.

Thank you dearest friends.

chapter one

an innocent beginning

Life in the late fifties in a small Scottish town was hard, as it was in the whole of Britain. Peace was only eleven years old when I was born on the 16th of February 1956 in the upstairs bedroom of my grandparents' farmhouse, Ancaster Cottage, on the edge of the small town of Callander in Perthshire, in the heart of Scotland.

My mother and the midwife were no doubt delighted to bring a baby boy into the world as Dad paced around at the bottom of the stairs – fathers weren't present at the birth in those days. I was born in the bedroom that I would share with my brother and two sisters.

We moved soon after I was born to a street called Willoughby Place, although we returned to Ancaster Cottage later. The houses there were prefabs, small temporary metal houses built after the war to meet the country's housing needs. They lasted many more years than intended. I remember ours being very much like a metal box inside, with slightly rounded corners, if I can put it that way. From the outside our house looked like a nice little cottage with a front door in the middle and two windows equally spaced either side and a straight path leading from it to the road.

Within about a year we had moved again, this time to number three Glen Gardens. Glen Gardens was all council houses then, the right to buy not yet existing, though no one could have afforded to anyway. It was a very smart street – the grass was cut and the gardens kept very tidy. On our side the gardens bordered the main Stirling to Oban railway line – literally only ten metres from our back door. We got used to the noise and smell of the huge steam trains thundering past. In fact they were a source of excitement to us children and, looking back, we were true railway children. A great part of our young lives revolved around the line. I'm surprised none of us were killed by a train – we used to clamber up the embankment at the end of the garden, through the fence and onto the line. There we would rest our heads on the line – you could hear a train coming for miles, or so we thought, although it sometimes appeared without warning, racing down the straight at high speed. As a train approached we would place a penny on the line and wait as two hundred tonnes of locomotive and carriages passed over the penny. There were dozens of pennies imprinted into the line on that stretch of railway, and in the early sixties a penny was a heck of a lot of money to a child – you could buy a McCowan's Dainty bar with one.

After only about a year we were on the move again, back to my grandparents' farmhouse, the place of my birth. My grandad moonlighted for British Rail and was the guardsman on the Stirling to Oban overnight mail train. He knew all the engine drivers so well that when the night train went past the farm the driver would toss great lumps of coal into the field from the tender. In the morning we would go down with wheelbarrows to collect it.

Going back to the farm was the start of another great adventure.

Ancaster Cottage was primarily a pig farm, and one of the biggest in Perthshire at the time. We also had a few cows and ponies and huge Clydesdale horses. There were hens too, and ducks and geese.

At five years old, it was time for me to start school. I remember my first day there, knowing that I was going to hate every minute of my school life. I believed that my carefree childhood was ending, but I had no idea why. However, as the days, weeks and months went on, I felt increasingly that I had been right. It seemed to me that, for no reason I could fathom, I was treated differently to the other children in the class by the teacher and sometimes by some of my male classmates. For the next two years this was the way it was. I was often bullied on the way home from school – we all had to walk home, some of us for a mile or more; nobody used cars to ferry children about in those days.

But the railway was always there and on the way home from school we would cross the railway bridge just as the 3.15 Callander to Stirling express came powering round the curve. We would all be hanging over the bridge parapet, looking down the engine's funnel as it passed below: there are some things in childhood you don't forget.

I loved living on the farm. Friends came over from the housing schemes and we just roamed around, feeding the hens or looking at the piglets. There was one Clydesdale horse in particular called Bridget – her job was to haul felled trees out of the forest for the wood cutters. Bridget was so well trained that I could make her sit, just like a dog, and climb on to her and ride her bareback, hanging on to her mane as she trotted round the field.

At the age of seven I was beginning to feel that something was going on. I realized then that I was different, although I didn't know in what way. I just knew I wasn't like other boys. I remember one day, when we were painting pictures in class, I was sharing a desk with a girl called Alison, and she said to me, 'You have very small hands – they're girls' hands.' I didn't know what to say, but I knew right there and then that I was happy about what she had just said, because I knew that a girl should have small hands. I didn't know where that thought came from, but from that moment I knew that my life would never be the same again. It was the moment that everything changed for me.

I couldn't stop thinking about what Alison had said. I realized that I didn't like playing football with the boys, didn't like playing conkers or playing kick the can in the playground. I preferred to watch what the girls were doing, though I never had the nerve to go over and join them. I suppose this made me a little bit of a loner at times, which didn't go unnoticed by the other kids or by the teachers.

At home, I was beginning to take an interest in my big sister's clothes. I would sneak into her bedroom and look at them and at her makeup on the dressing table, and think, 'Why can't I be like this?' Soon, I graduated to trying on some of my sister's clothes and it felt so right to me, but I still couldn't understand why. Mum caught me one day and told Dad, and later on that day they told me there must be something wrong with me and that I would have to go to the doctor. I started crying because I didn't want to go to the doctor when I didn't feel ill, but they never made me go and nothing more was said about it. This was the start of a lifelong trend where no one would face up to my differences or attempt to understand me because no one knew how to deal with me.

At school the teachers just didn't know how to respond to an eight-year-old boy who was so different. One teacher in particular, Miss Moffat, an old dragon and very old fashioned, made my life hell for a whole year. She put me down at every opportunity, and when it came to class work, if I asked for help she would come over to my desk and slap the back of my hand with a ruler and tell me to get on with it or else. I was left handed and she tried to force me into using my right hand, though at eight years old, thankfully, I won that battle. I knew there was no point complaining, so I bore the brunt of her victimization, but I firmly believe to this day that she was responsible for my less than impressive performance at school from then on, and the end result was that she stripped me of the little confidence that I had. I was also too scared to tell my parents for fear that they wouldn't have believed me. Sadly, situations where I would be discriminated against and victimized are something that have followed me throughout my life.

But it wasn't all bad. During the 1960s, Callander was the backdrop to a world-famous TV programme, Dr Finlay's Casebook – one of the early TV soaps. The town was known in the series as Tannochbrae, and tourists still come to take photos of the doctor's house to this day. The programme makers needed a number of school children for the filming and I was lucky enough to be chosen, so I became a part-time child actor for a while. It was a release from my classroom troubles, and we were paid – one ten-shilling note, a box of toffees and a fish and chip dinner at a local hotel for each episode that you were in: an absolute fortune. I still have the ten-bob note from the final episode that I appeared in.

I still had three years to do at primary school. I was finally out of Miss Moffat's class, but my next teacher, Mrs Hinchcliff, was no better. She seemed to have some special kind of contempt for me and would stare and snarl at me for no reason at all and just wouldn't allow me to progress in any way. She terrified me for a whole year.

I would come to realize over the years that the very people who could have helped or advised me, such as teachers, doctors, workmates and friends, were usually the very people who would be downright nasty and horrible to me. The bullying on the way home from school continued. They didn't punch or kick me, but they would throw me about between them, pushing me to the ground until I cried. I never ever tried to run away though, as I thought it would be worse the next time, and I definitely couldn't tell the teacher.

I knew this for sure when I was in primary six, so I was only ten or eleven at the time. I was walking along the cloakroom corridor when I saw a member of staff coming towards me who had kids at our school. When our paths crossed he suddenly launched himself at me, pinning me to the wall amongst the coat hangers, placing his hand over my face and forcing my head against the wall, saying angrily, 'Keep away from my kids, you little queer. I don't want you talking to them, got it? And if you do I will make sure you're expelled. Do you understand?'

I tried to answer, but was so terrified I couldn't get the words out. He then just cast me aside and stormed off, turning round, pointing and saying, 'Remember what I said, or else.' The whole episode left me totally terrified and traumatised and I still struggle with my memory of it to this day. The really upsetting thing for me at the time was that I couldn't understand why my teachers were treating me like this because I'd done nothing wrong. I was just a very confused wee kid.

School holidays always came round again, and it was back to the great adventure of the farm and the railway. As I said earlier, my grandad was the guard on the overnight mail train to Oban and it was on one of those journeys in 1964 that he befriended two of the regular passengers on the train: Mr and Mrs McKinnon from the Isle of Coll. We had never heard of the island and didn't know where it was. But as time went on, Grandad got friendlier and friendlier with the McKinnons until eventually they invited us all over to the island for our next summer holiday. It was 1965. We squeezed into Dad's Hillman Minx at two in the morning and drove to Oban to catch the boat which left at 5.30 a.m. We didn't know what to expect as we lived in central Scotland, about as far away from the sea as you could get, so we were nervous as we boarded what seemed like a pretty large ship to us.

As time went on we came to love the ship, the Claymore, very much. She took a full four hours to reach the Isle of Coll. The island was a stark contrast to the inland town we had come from, but we grew to love it too, even if it didn't have any trees or any electricity at the time.

Our new friend, Duncan McKinnon, was the farm manager at Gallanach Farm, very different to our farm back home in Callander. Gallanach had beaches, sand dunes and strange-sounding birds in the fields – corncrakes that kept us awake at night. Duncan and Margaret had two children about our age called John and Mary. We all became close friends and we treated their parents like our aunty and uncle. For the next five years all our family holidays were on the Isle of Coll. In the mid-1960s the island didn't get many tourists, just a few bird watchers and the Coll exiles who returned to their family homes for the summer – early summer swallows as they are known nowadays.

Our arrival would spread round the island like wildfire, and people would come up to us and say, 'We heard you were coming', which made us feel special, almost like celebrities. In return, the McKinnons would come to our farm for their holidays and Duncan would plough some of our fields – a busman's holiday. But times and lives change, and 1970 was our last family holiday on the Isle of Coll. I wouldn't return until fifteen years later, in 1985.

Although I had realized from the age of seven that I was different, by the age of twelve I still had no real idea what was happening to me. For all I knew I could have been the only kid in the entire world who felt like me, or maybe half the kids in the world did and I just hadn't met them yet. The fact was, I just didn't know. I thought this was just the way life was. Little did I know that things were about to get a whole lot more complicated.

chapter two

a very mixed-up teenager

Although my childhood years were troubled, they were fundamentally happy. My brother, two sisters and I had a good home life. Mum and Dad worked hard and although there wasn't a lot of money, we were well looked after and had everything we needed. If we wanted something we had to earn it – a principle that would stand me in good stead in the coming years for the challenges that lay ahead.

At Easter, for example, when most kids would get chocolate eggs, we would be sent down to where the geese had laid their eggs and would gather one for every member of the family. They were about three times the size of hens' eggs and we would hard boil them and paint faces on them. On Easter Sunday we would roll them down the hill at the back of the house. We would then have them for lunch – you didn't waste anything in those days.

Although we were quite close and got on well with each other, we were not the type of family that discussed things, so some issues were just not talked about – either by us kids, amongst ourselves, or between Mum and Dad, and that was certainly true when it came to my issues, which were starting to affect the whole family.

*

By the age of nine I was crying myself to sleep most nights, but the odd thing was that I would still be crying when I woke in the morning, and the really scary part was that apparently I would cry through the night and could not be wakened by Mum and Dad. When my mum took me to the doctor he just said that I would grow out of it. This did happen after about a year or so – the doctor really hadn't known what the cause was and, unfortunately, it would be something that would affect me again, many years later.

I would soon be leaving primary school – a day that I was eagerly awaiting. The bad news, though, was that I would be going to high school at the end of the summer holidays. All I could think about right then was the dreadful experiences I'd had at primary school. McLaren High School was a daunting prospect – it had over seven hundred pupils, which, to me, represented a very large number of potential bullies. However, it turned out that the fact there were so many children worked, in some ways, to my advantage.

I was also about to become a teenager and, like most other kids of that age, I was having thoughts of an increasingly sexual nature. All the boys seemed to be talking about girls and of course the girls were talking about boys, which left me somewhere in the middle. Sometimes I leaned one way, sometimes the other, and it was beginning to tear me apart. But there was one thing I did know for sure and that was that I wasn't gay. Of course, 'gay' wasn't the word that was used in those days, but I definitely knew I wasn't 'one of them'. If I liked a boy I did so because, at that particular moment, I really felt that I was a girl.

The first boy I really fancied was Davy Jones of the Monkees. I was infatuated with him. The Monkees' TV show was on at 4 p.m.

on a Saturday afternoon, and we used to watch it as a family. Although I was watching it primarily to drool over Davy, I was also interested in the drummer in the band, not because I fancied him too, but to watch him play the drums. Drums would very soon become a big part of my life. Around this time my uncle Roy, who lived with us then, came home one day with a single snare drum. He said that his friend Tony had given him it saying, 'Would the wee fellow like this?' and he plonked it down in front of me. I started playing around with it and found that I took to it quite quickly, and soon I was playing along to my big sister's Beatles records. Even with just the one drum I was making some kind of half-decent rhythm with it, and I remember the first tune I mastered being *Love Me Do*.

Drumming also gave me a great excuse to go into my sister's bedroom on the pretext of looking for another record to practise to, I would do this, but I would also nick some items of clothing from the bottom of her drawer that I thought she wouldn't realize were missing, as the urge to build up my stock of female clothing was becoming stronger. The problem then was where to hide the stuff and I went to some elaborate lengths to conceal it. The hay barn was my favourite hiding place, and I even used to get dressed up in there because I knew I could hide among the hay bales if I heard someone coming.

However, Mum was becoming suspicious and always seemed to know when I was in the hay barn although it took me a while to work out how she knew. We had a family of farm cats that kept the rats down – which was important because we had hens and pigs – and although they were semi-wild, one kitten had befriended me. So it became my cat and it didn't like anyone else. I was allowed to have it in the house like a normal pet and it would follow me everywhere. And that's how Mum knew I was in the barn a lot – the cat was regularly sitting outside the door waiting for me, unwittingly advertising the fact that I was in there.

In 1968, as in previous years, most of the summer holiday was spent on the Isle of Coll. Strangely, I found that when I was there my mixed-up thoughts about my gender issues largely disappeared. Life on Coll was such a profound contrast to life in Central Scotland that it engulfed me completely and all my little worries and issues disappeared while I was there. To this day I can't explain why this happened although I still meet people who tell me similar tales of coming to Coll and escaping their problems. This would also be the case on our next two holidays to the island, and was something that would recur many years later.

But the dreaded first day at high school was fast approaching. It was much further away from home than primary school had been – getting on for two miles away – and I was particularly worried about the walk home, as the route went through a narrow leafy lane called the Creek. This was a place to be avoided at night; it was there that those who had bullied me at primary school could easily ambush me. I also had to cross the river by going over one of two bridges, and I was worried someone would throw me into the river just for fun.

I did have a female friend at school who knew that I sometimes wore female clothes. She had a boyfriend who was from a neighbouring town and therefore hadn't been at our primary school, but the children from all the surrounding villages came to our secondary school. He was really tough and had a fearsome reputation. No one would cross him, even the prefects were scared of him and I'm sure some of the teachers were too. My friend told me that if I wanted, she would ask him to deal with the boys who had been bullying me at primary school. Although I told her that I didn't want any one to get hurt over me, even though they had terrorized me for six years, she said not to worry she would sort things out, and while I don't know what her boyfriend said to them, the bullies didn't bother me ever again and would actually avoid me at all costs. This protection was slightly confusing for me, though, as he would also laugh at me because he knew that I wore girls' clothes sometimes. I guess my friend must have told him.

As had been a pretty frequent feature of our family life, we were on the move again. It was 1969 and Grandad was getting too old to work the farm while Dad and my uncle Roy were too busy doing other things. They were both quite entrepreneurial – as well as working the farm with Grandad and working as a fireman, Dad was also a timber contractor, and Uncle Roy had bought a JCB digger and gone into that line of work too. I can't ever remember Mum having a job anywhere, but she was a bit of a high flyer in local politics and held many posts on the town council over the years.

I suppose it was a sign of the times when Mum and Dad decided to sell the farmhouse and all the land to property developers, the result being that in just a few years' time hundreds of houses were built on the land that had played such a big part in our childhood. This increased the size of the town considerably, but thankfully the farmhouse is still there. Whenever I go back to Callander I walk past the house and usually become very emotional – but also very happy when I think about my carefree childhood on that farm.

When we sold the farm Mum and Dad bought the recently closed down Royal & Commercial Bank building in Main Street, Callander. They completely refurbished it and turned it into a hotel which they named after Mum's favourite place on the Isle of Coll – a tiny hamlet called Sorisdale, at the east end of the island.

As I grew up I found it ever more difficult to deal with my gender conflict, now fast becoming a crisis which dominated my thoughts every minute of every day. I would go to sleep at night thinking about it and I would wake up every morning still thinking about it. Moving to the hotel was quite helpful, though, since for the first time in my life I had my own bedroom, and every single moment I was in my room I would dress up in female clothes. I had now become quite skilled at applying makeup, too, and as far as I was concerned, I looked and felt pretty hot. I would nervously venture out onto the hotel landing as guests were coming and going, fervently hoping that they would just see a young girl.

I think I got away with it most of the time, except for one awful occasion when Grandad appeared at the top of the stairs and saw me. I shot back into my room, and when I saw him later that day he asked, 'What was that all about?' I told him that I had had a girlfriend with me and it was her he had seen. I don't think I got away with that one, though, and our relationship became quite strained after that. But I also don't think he said anything to Mum and Dad and eventually we resumed a normal relationship, of sorts. From then on we had this kind of awkward understanding where I knew that he knew, and he knew that I knew that he knew. It was something we never ever discussed.

I had learned from a young age that the only way to get what you wanted was to make it happen yourself, through hard work and perseverance – no one was going to just come along and hand you anything on a plate. So, by the age of fourteen I had already done a variety of jobs, and with only about a year to go before I left school I was already on the lookout for the right full-time position. I had saved up about £250 in a savings account at the Bank of Scotland and I wanted to spend some of it, but I also wanted to earn money from whatever it was that I bought, so that's when I got my first set of drums. I reckoned, like most kids of my age at the time, that I was going to be a rock star someday. The drums cost me £65 and all I had to do now was learn how to play really well.

Living in the hotel had its benefits. Loads of interesting people came into the very busy bar downstairs, including musicians. There was one in particular – his name was Arthur Eason and his nickname was Peen (I never found out what that meant). It was widely accepted in the music business that he was the best Scottish dance band drummer on the planet. He had played with all the top Scottish bands of the day, including Jimmy Shand, Jimmy Blue and the Ian Powrie Band, to name but a few, and he was a regular guest on light entertainment television programmes at that time. He also did session work and had toured the world extensively with many famous bands. And here he was, drinking in my dad's pub! The problem was that he drank far too much and he was falling from grace in the music business because of it. He was becoming so unreliable that he just wasn't getting the work any more, and that's why he spent all his time in Dad's pub. This was definitely a stroke of luck as far as I was concerned, however: now all I had to do was persuade him to teach me to play the drums.

Although I was only fourteen, I used to float in and out of the bar – not drinking of course, just cruising through – and one particular day I plucked up the courage to ask Arthur if he would give me some drum lessons. To my surprise he said yes, but the next big question I had was how much would it cost me, bearing in mind he really was the world's finest Scottish dance band drummer. Well, he said he'd come upstairs and give me a half-hour lesson every time he came into the pub, which was of course every day. He said all I had to do was make sure he had enough to drink. He drank Carlsberg Special Brew and it usually cost me two bottles per session – not bad for drum lessons from one of the world's greatest drummers, even if he was half-pissed most of the time! After about six months I had become quite proficient at Scottish dance music drumming, thanks to Arthur (Peen) Eason and around two hundred bottles of Special Brew.

However, it was an encounter with another musician who was booked to play in the bar on the first Friday of the month that would give me my first break on the road to what I dreamed would be superstardom. He was a top accordion player called Mel McLaren. I was keen to hear any live music and Dad had said I could sit in the bar and listen whenever there was live music on. On this particular night, when it came to Mel's halftime break, he came over to me and said, 'I hear you've been getting drum lessons from Peen – he tells me you've become very proficient and says you're ready to do gigs.'

I replied, 'Well, if Peen says so, I must be!'

As soon as I said that, he said, 'I'm looking for a young fresh drummer for my band – would you be interested?'

I immediately said yes, and then, 'But don't you want to hear me play first?'

He just said, 'If Peen says you're good, that's good enough for me. All we need is a rehearsal before your first gig.' So, at age fourteen I played my first gig in the Port of Menteith village hall, and I was paid £4. I had hit the big time.

At last I had turned fifteen, and with the start of the summer holidays I would be leaving school. I just couldn't wait, as my ten years of education had been nothing short of a nightmare. The persecution I had suffered from teachers and pupils alike had almost driven me to breaking point many times, and somewhat surprisingly, the primary school teachers were the worst. I still don't understand how they could have been so nasty to an innocent child. I still feel sick at the thought of Miss Moffat treating me as if I was some sort of freak.

Although my experience at high school was marginally better because no one dared to openly bully me for fear of what my friend's boyfriend might do to them, I was still persecuted by other pupils and some teachers – it was just done a little more subtly. Once I got 95% for a technical drawing exam, which, I admit, was much better than I would normally have done and our techie teacher made me stand up in front of the whole class and said to me, 'Well, we all thought you were the village idiot, but you've pulled it out of the bag this time – but wouldn't you be better doing knitting or sewing, or home economics even? Wouldn't that suit you better?' At which point, with a huge condescending smile on his face, he beckoned the whole class to react to his joke and they duly obliged with instantaneous laughter and derogatory taunting remarks.

Our history teacher hated me with a passion, for no other reason I can think of than that he must have known about me; I wasn't disruptive in class or anything like that – in fact, I kept my head down and tried to get on; I quite liked history. He had decided that he wasn't going to use my proper name either, and christened me 'Owl', saying, 'Or is it brown owl? Because you should be in the Brownies.'

Throughout my school days it was teachers who actively victimized me at every opportunity and in fact fed off each other, and this in turn encouraged my fellow pupils to follow suit. Can you imagine this sort of thing happening today? No, I don't think so. But this was the 1970s, a different era.

Finally the big day came. It was my last few hours at school and I had never been so excited about anything in my life – well, apart from when Davy Jones of the Monkees appeared on TV on a Saturday afternoon. When that final bell rang and the whole class made a dash for the door, I felt a ton weight lifting from my shoulders. I let most of the others go ahead of me and as I went out into the corridor and saw them all charging towards the stairs, I could see this chapter of my struggle disappearing into the past. I made my way out into the school yard and broke down in tears as I headed for the gates – my sense of total relief was so overwhelming. Once I was clear of the gates I was fine again. I looked at the road ahead and wondered where it would take me. I decided there and then that it would take me wherever I wanted it to. Even so, subconsciously I knew that this new chapter of my life probably wasn't going to be any easier than the last, and that a rocky road lay ahead.

After the annual summer holiday to the Isle of Coll in 1971, which was our last as a family, I was set to start my first full-time job, again, thanks to customers of Mum and Dad's pub. There was a bakery just along the road and the bakers were pub regulars. I'm not sure who, but Mum or Dad had mentioned that I would soon be leaving school and asked the owner if there were there any jobs going. He said they needed an apprentice and that I could have the job, and I could start the very next week. I decided to accept and my starting wage was £7 for forty hours per week. I was also getting £4 per gig playing the drums in the dance band, doing two or three gigs a week, so I suddenly felt extremely well off. Yes, it did seem like I'd really hit the big time!

The early 1970s were an extremely exciting time for me and the friends I still had from my school days. It was the glam rock era, with groups like T-Rex, Sweet, Slade, Wizzard, Mud, David Bowie, Alice Cooper and many more, and that was right up my street. What excited me most was that all these bands wore makeup, platform shoes, dangly earrings, tight glittery trousers and just about everything feminine you could think of. So, of course, as fans we copied them, and for me this was great. Wearing platform shoes felt like wearing high heels in public although no one knew the real reason why I loved them so much.

As the 70s wore on, I found it harder and harder to suppress my longing to dress up as a female and I did so at every opportunity. My family definitely knew I was up to something, but nothing was ever said – it was just too awkward for them to talk about. I knew Mum looked in my room for clues and I suspect she probably found them – quite often she would be really off with me for days on end. It must have been really hard for her to know how to deal with me, given her suspicions. This situation drifted on for years and it must have been heart-breaking for her to see her son carrying on the way I did, when she couldn't even begin to comprehend why.

At that time there was very little understanding of people with my kind of complicated issues – indeed, even I still didn't really know what I was and whether I was alone in the world, or if there were others like me – there was just no way of finding out. I didn't even know at that time if there was a name for what I was. I hadn't noticed anyone else with the tell-tale signs, and I certainly couldn't have talked to anyone about it. But the not-knowing was becoming absolutely unbearable. With the pressure of having to conceal what I was doing becoming more and more unbearable, I had begun to cry myself to sleep again, and I could only live my female life in the confines of my bedroom. However, at the age of seventeen I passed my driving test, which opened up a whole new world to me and gave me the freedom to spread my female wings.

Now I could escape the confines of my home town. I could go to any city I chose and be totally anonymous – I could go out onto busy city centre streets fully dressed as a female and no one would know me. This was liberation and I made the most of it! I could never have risked doing that on the streets of Callander; no matter how well I was made up, people there had known me all my life and would have recognized me.

Additionally, I could also spread my wings in the music world. I had now been playing drums on the local Scottish dance band scene for about three years, and it had been a real education in the fundamentals of playing in a band; laying down the bedrock of my understanding of how each member of any band had their part to play – not least the drummer whose rock-steady rhythm and impeccable timing was what held the whole band together. If the drummer messed up the whole band messed up. Another thing I learned about playing in a band was that we worked hard, but we also socialized very hard. This meant drinking a great deal and was something I was just learning to do, but I soon got the hang of it. I suppose it was inevitable that I would move on from the Scottish dance band scene, and around this time I said goodbye to my early band mentors who had pointed me in the right direction – particularly big Mel McLaren. I now had my sights set on playing in pop and rock bands. Yes, I still thought I was heading for superstardom – and in some ways I was.

I had by now been working in the bakery for about three years and was attending Falkirk Technical College where I was taking a City & Guilds qualification in bakery and confectionery. Falkirk was a one-and-a-half-hour bus journey each way, three days a week, and I was the only person who attended from my neck of the woods – all the other students were from the Falkirk area. I was therefore already the odd one out, and some of the lads thought I was a bit on the feminine side too.

College was beginning to feel a bit like the bad old school days as people were starting to ridicule me. I had recently begun to shave the hair from my arms and chest and this was obviously noticed. I remember one of my fellow students coming over to the hotplate where I was busy making pancakes one day and touching my arm with a very hot pallet knife. He said, 'That should remove the hairs from your arms, you fucking poof.' My instinctive reaction was to push him away, which didn't go down well. Of course, like many others, before and after him, he had got me completely wrong – I was not gay at all – but that was how he and his friends saw me. At this point the tutor, Mr Middledich, stepped in and broke it up. After class I was summoned to his office and asked what was going on because he could see I was upset. I told him the whole story and said that I was too scared to continue with my course and wouldn't be coming back. At this point he said he would see what he could do to help me finish the course some other way and told me he would be in touch with my boss at the bakery.

Just as I had felt during those bad old days at school when I was being bullied, I was once again worried about the walk home after class – though in this case it was the walk back to the bus station. At the end of the day I walked briskly out of college, heading for the bus station. Once there I thought I would be safe as there were lots of people around. However, I was wrong. The gang of boys from college suddenly appeared and the one who had burned me with the knife walked straight up to me and head-butted me right between the eyes. He floored me and blood gushed from my nose, at which point they all fled, laughing, as onlookers came to my assistance. The physical pain and the two black eyes I was left with were bad enough, but it was the psychological effect that was harder to deal with. I kept thinking, 'Why have they done this to me? I've done nothing to them, they don't know what I'm going through. Why are some people so cruel to me?' I felt utterly isolated.

Thankfully, a couple of weeks later the college arranged for me to do the remainder of my course from home and I only had to attend college to take the practical exams which I was allowed to take on my own. This arrangement worked really well and I did eventually get my qualifications.

My move from playing drums in Scottish dance bands to playing with pop-rock groups was partly driven by the idea that I could perhaps get away with wearing makeup and feminine clothing, at least while on stage, like the glam rock bands I loved and admired, and no one would work out my real reasons for dressing up. I had long hair anyway, which was very common at the time, and my plan worked quite well in the coming years.

My huge and increasingly powerful desire to be female was something I could never ever contemplate sharing with anyone. I call it desire because I didn't know it was anything else at that time. It still hadn't occurred to me that how I felt could be a condition or perhaps even an illness. Although my family kind of knew, they would never have mentioned it to anyone either, for fear of possible ridicule coming to their door.

I went to extraordinary lengths to conceal what I was doing and used to hide female clothes inside my drum cases, in the hope that Mum wouldn't find them there. I had joined a local pop group called Magnum Force, and I remember playing a gig one night in Denny, in central Scotland. At the time I would stash clothes in all manner of places and unfortunately, on that particular evening I had forgotten all about the ladies clothes I had hidden in my drum cases. When I unpacked my drum kit on stage at the gig and lifted the lids off the drum cases, all everyone could see was girls' clothes. I felt a cold sweat break out on my forehead and panicking, I wondered how I was ever going to explain myself. In a split second I came up with the idea that I would tell the band this was my new gimmick, and I proceeded to hang tights, blouses and other garments from my microphone and cymbal stands. But I'm sure no one really fell for that story; yet again no one wanted to broach the subject because they didn't really know for sure what I was doing. And as far as Mum was concerned, I don't think it would have mattered what I did to conceal my girly paraphernalia; she more or less knew what I was doing anyway. I'm sure she knew where I hid it, most of the time.

A perfect example of Mum knowing what I was doing was the time I had a couple of weeks off from all of my commitments. I decided that I might be able to kill two birds with one stone and I packed all my gear, including my drum kit and a selection of female clothing, into my Ford Escort estate and headed to Blackpool where I had made a couple of enquiries with a music agent and had secured some band work. I also knew that Blackpool was a very busy and fast-moving place where I could probably fit in as a female when I was not drumming. Everything worked out very well for the couple of weeks that I was there. I did some gigs as a boy and when I wasn't on stage I spent the rest of my time as a girl which was fantastic. For the first time in my life I was able to dress how I wanted for more than a few hours at any one time and I found the freedom exhilarating.

However, after I got back home, Mum said to me, 'I know what you were doing in Blackpool.' Strangely, I found that now it was me avoiding the situation, although I still cannot say why. I just accepted that she knew what I was up to, though to this day I have no idea how she knew what I had been doing. It may be that she knew where I hid my female stuff in my bedroom and saw that it was missing, but I don't know for sure.

I was beginning to feel a major conflict between my female side and my male side, and this was something that would, for many years, be one of my most difficult struggles. This struggle would cause me to make serious errors of judgement and do things that I just didn't want to do; all to try and prove to others that I wasn't who I actually was – the person my mind was trying to tell me I was, the person I would continue to run away from for many more years to come.

chapter three

years of denial

My innocent childhood, with its mixture of happiness and troubled times, was long gone, replaced by mixed-up heady teenage years of excitement, ambition, optimism for the great challenge of the future that lay ahead of me. But my spirit was becoming increasingly stifled by the realization that what my mind was telling me wasn't what was expected of me in this world; a world where a person was expected to behave the way the majority did, and it was at this time my inner conflict began in earnest although it was very subtle and unconscious at first.

I thoroughly enjoyed becoming a nameless female on the rare occasions when I could escape from my daily life, but the conflict that was slowly building up within me would lead me to try and draw away from my feminine side and begin to do more and more of those things that a young man was expected to do, like going to the pub with my mates, just to fit in. The female part of me would then tug and tug and pull me back, again and again. It was just like the ebb and flow of the tide, and this conflict would continue for the next twenty-eight years, gradually becoming much more dramatic and sometimes even violent.

Towards the end of the 1970s I still hadn't realized that I might be in some sort of denial. I did decide, though, that the baker's life wasn't for me. Very early mornings – a 5 a.m. start on weekdays and 3 a.m. on Saturdays – were not compatible with my life on the road with the various bands I now played in. My male side was telling me that I should be doing something else, and that's when I got a job working in a quarry. It was totally male dominated except for the girl in the weighbridge office. I did put up with the job for some years because the company was sympathetic to my requests for time off to go and play in the various bands that I was involved with, and the money was brilliant. What I just couldn't stand was the derogatory way that some of my workmates would talk about their wives or girlfriends and women in general. There was nothing sinister or nasty, but every man bragged about how they dominated their partners and how they could do whatever they liked while their women had to stay at home and pander to their every need. I found these attitudes very hard to deal with and I hated the way they all tried to outdo each other all the time. Dealing with their chauvinistic attitudes would be the trigger for my female side to gain the upper hand again. It was almost like a protest against my male workmates and consequently against any maleness within myself.

For most of the time I worked in the quarry I led a totally double life. If the guys had ever found out what I was doing, my life wouldn't have been worth living. That said, one of my workmates actually did discover my secret. Luckily for me he was my best friend. I would often go to his house for a drink with him and his wife – we even cycled to work together, and did all the stuff that mates do.

My family and I had recently moved from the hotel to a big

house on the edge of town, quite close to the main road, and one weekend I was in the house alone and decided to get made up as a female and go out for the night in Edinburgh. Just as I was getting into my car my friend drove past and immediately spotted me. I just knew by the look on his face that he had put two and two together and that I'd been rumbled for sure. Although I went to Edinburgh as planned, I couldn't eat, sleep or do anything for the rest of the weekend, worrying about what would await me when I got to work on Monday morning. I fully expected to be ridiculed, or worse, by all the men in the quarry. Surprisingly, this didn't happen and just like the time Grandad had caught me dressed up in the hotel, James never ever mentioned he'd seen me all dressed up. Although relations were a bit strained between us for a while, they eventually got back to something like normal after a few weeks. But, just like Grandad, I knew that he knew, and he knew that I knew he knew.

The tug of war between my male and female sides continued to dominate my life and my doubts about which gender I really was were becoming ever stronger. I would have wild swings one way or the other, and would sometimes feel totally male or totally female for months on end. And during one of my male periods, when I was in the Ancaster pub in Callander with my workmates, I met someone who would completely change my life. Her name was Anne and she was one of the staff there. I got talking to her and we hit it off right away.

She was one of the countless girls who had come from Glasgow to work in the many hotels in the town which catered for the thousands of tourists who flocked to the area every year. We started seeing each other on a regular basis and as the months went on things became much more serious between us. It really was quite a happy time, but eventually my female side started to rise again, causing me to swing back that way once more. This was now even more problematic than before because I had become very fond of Anne – perhaps it may even have become more than that by this time. However, I had led something of a double life since my early teens and I reckoned there was no reason why I couldn't continue with this, even with Anne on board. I just didn't want to let her go, so for the first time in my life I was seeing two women at the same time – one was Anne and the other was the still-nameless female that I had become.

As time went on Anne and I became ever closer, and although I had thought this would never happen to me in my complicated life, I realized that I was head over heels in love, and that Anne was in love with me too. Deep down, though, I knew our relationship would just make life all the more complicated for me, and, sadly, for Anne too. Trying to lead my double life and have a girlfriend at the same time, I knew it was inevitable that I would be caught out sooner or later.

When Anne worked evening shifts at the hotel I had time to go out as the female I had become. Around this time, too, I was also becoming increasingly busy playing in bands, and although Anne didn't always know exactly what I was doing at nights, she always wanted to see me when I got back home and she often commented that I looked different – even after I had washed all the makeup off my face.

After a while she realised that something was up and asked me what was going on. To begin with I pretended I didn't know what she was talking about, but after a few weeks of her constant questioning, I decided to tell her everything. I thought, well she'll either stay with me or she'll just leave. As it turned out, she stayed. I suppose she must have loved me very much, but although she put up with what I was doing, she didn't want to know any details and she turned a blind eye to behaviour that must have seemed out of place to her. Thinking about it now, I realise that I was extremely selfish thinking I could have the best of both worlds and get away with it indefinitely.

Something that I could never have foreseen did come of my telling Anne my secret. I remember she was getting ready to go to work one night, soon after I had bared my soul to her, and she asked me what I was doing that night.

I said, 'Oh, I don't know', and she replied, 'I suppose you're going out with Julie.'

I said, 'Who?' and she said, 'You know who I mean. Julie.'

From that moment on the nameless female within me had a name. My name was Julie and I just loved it.

I did have the best of both worlds for years, but Anne's acceptance would wax and wane and we fell out over my double life many times. I suppose I knew deep down that this situation could not go on for ever, but it would be many years before things would come to a head.

Peculiarly, around that time, after so many years of not knowing what these feelings were that seemed to be consuming my whole life, I was soon to hear about a strange-sounding condition that seemed to be exactly what I was suffering from. I was watching television on my own one night and a Michael Caine movie began. I'm pretty sure it was one of the Harry Palmer series, although unfortunately I have so far been unable to track down the specific episode.

Michael Caine played a private investigator and in this one he followed some guy around Europe on trains to different cities, staying in different hotels. He had to search the guy's room, including his suitcase, which turned out to be full of women's clothes, wigs and everything else that a female impersonator might have. At this point Michael says, 'I've been had! This guy's a fake, a transvestite!'

Wow, I had never even heard this word before and it shocked me to the core. I went straight over to the bookcase and looked it up in the dictionary. I just couldn't get the word out of my head for weeks, and I went on for many years after that thinking that this is what I was – a transvestite. As time went on I would find out that I was not a transvestite, but something much more complicated than that. However, at that time I thought I had some sort of an answer to who, or what, I was.

I was still working in the quarry and had joined a new band. It was what I can only describe as a mid-Atlantic country rock band, playing a mixture of country rock and pop music from both sides of the Atlantic with a little bit of Scottish music thrown in. The band was called Merlin's Dream, and it was one of the most successful bands I had played in – both creatively and financially. We were making a bundle and securing so many bookings that it was putting a strain on other aspects of my life, such as my day job and my relationship with Anne – as well as, of course, with the other woman in my life, now named Julie. The gigs were coming in so fast that we decided to embark on a world tour – although our world only extended from Inverness in the north to Dumfries in the south! But it felt like the world to us; we played to many nationalities: Scandinavian oil workers in the north east,

American navy personnel at the Clyde Naval bases, and European forces personnel at the NATO base at Machrihanish on the Mull of Kintyre, as well as playing the working men's clubs in towns all over Scotland.

The training I had received in the early days when I played in the Scottish dance band was now paying off – I was a good musician and knew how to perform on stage, and I also knew how to socialize after the gigs. All those stories about sex, drugs and rock and roll are definitely true! For myself, I can say truthfully that I didn't do the sex or the drugs, but I did do a lot of drinking and got into all kinds of crazy carryings on – I was a drummer, after all. I think there's a wee bit of Keith Moon in many drummers – there certainly was in me at the time.

I didn't do the sex because my confusion over my gender just wouldn't let me. If I did hook up with a girl I would get to the point of jumping into bed with her and then suddenly think, this is not right. It wasn't right because in my head I saw myself as being the same as her, and I just couldn't go through with it, not ever. The lads in the band would say to me, 'You had it handed to you on a plate, what's wrong with you?' and I would make the excuse that I was being loyal to my girlfriend. In a way I was – and they would all laugh at me. I think they would probably have laughed a lot louder had they known the real reason for my celibacy. Although I had started a relationship with Anne for all the right reasons, at a period when my male side was more dominant than my female side, I always found our sexual relationship very difficult and would make up all sorts of excuses to avoid sex. I did make a few half-hearted attempts, especially in the early days, but I felt it was just wrong, as even then I saw the real me as a heterosexual female. Consequently, Anne was starved of sex for most of the time that we were together.

I didn't do drugs either, although only after giving it a go; being in the band I was expected to try it. It was nothing heavy – the others were smoking grass, so I tried it in the van on the way to a gig in Prestwick one day. It really didn't do much for me and I was never tempted to try it again. The lads laughed at me again, but I just said, 'I'll stick to the booze – that does plenty for me.'

When they smoked the stuff they would giggle like schoolchildren in the back of the van. They would even smoke during our breaks in the middle of gigs – they said it made them play better; I wasn't so sure about that. And of course this would continue wherever we were staying for the night. The guys used to do this weird thing that they called a nose blast – one of them would inhale a huge amount from a joint, and then exhale up the nose of the guy next to him. I had never seen anything like it in my life. I didn't get it then and I don't get it now – the whole drugs thing will forever be a mystery to me.

I should make it clear that the lads in the band weren't a load of junkies – they all had day jobs and families, and just took drugs recreationally. I don't even think they indulged during the week, and I suppose that's why they went a bit mad on the weekends when we were away with the band. I still don't get it though.

What with work, the band, a girlfriend and living this double life where I had to get my fix of being female, I had loads of friends and acquaintances. But apart from my girlfriend, I didn't really have a friend I could share my secret with at this point. I wasn't interested in football and the like and often didn't join my mates so eventually they involved me less and less in their activities. This made me stronger and much more determined to listen to what my mind was telling me and to persevere with what I wanted to do, not what others thought I should do. My determination increased in leaps and bounds, along with my belief in who and what I was, and for the very first time I was starting to look at my dilemma in a subtly different way. I was tentatively beginning to think I had the wrong body, as it was in total conflict with what was going through my mind. Externally I was a man, but everything inside me was saying woman.

My frequent trips, as Julie, to the cities in the central belt of Scotland continued and were great; I could walk along a busy high street or into a big shopping mall with thousands of people and just be anonymous – one of the crowd, shopping like any other female. All I wanted to be was an ordinary woman, nothing fancy, nothing sexy, I just wanted to fit in.

It was during such a trip, in one of the various nightspots that I used to go to in Edinburgh as Julie, that I would meet someone who would again change my life significantly. On this particular night I was in a bar down near Leith docks, dressed as Julie of course, and I was sitting near a table of about five or six people. Seeing I was on my own, they asked me if I'd like to join them. I hesitantly said yes, in my best female voice, and duly joined them. Over the course of the evening we hit it off and all bought each other drinks. I ended up getting on very well with one girl in particular, called Sue.

As the night went on she snuggled up to me and said quietly, 'Are you a tranny?'

I said, 'Tranny, what's that?'

She then repeated the question, saying, 'Are you a transvestite?'

I hesitated slightly and said nervously, 'Oh, yes, I suppose I am', and thought to myself, oh well, that will be the end of this friendship then.

Far from it – from that moment on she took me under her wing. We became close friends and would meet up every time Julie went to Edinburgh. Sue taught me much about the ways of being a modern city chick. It was a very exciting time and made me feel so confident. Over the next few years we became ever closer girlfriends and I was totally accepted by everyone in Sue's circle of friends. I didn't realize it at the time, but she was to leave me a wonderful life-changing legacy many years later, in early 2004.

chapter four

running away from the inevitable

The 1980s turned out to be the defining decade in my struggle to decide what my eventual gender would be – or rather, what my gender really was in the first place. During these turbulent years my life would swing, sometimes violently, between my male and female sides, but generally my male side dominated 75% of the time.

Since I was seven years old I had known I was different to other boys. I had evolved from simply looking at my sister's clothes in her room to travelling around, fully dressed and made up as a female. I had now come to the point where I thought I couldn't take this aspect of my life any further; I was just doing the same thing over and over again. It was during the 80s that my male side regained the high ground again and for some years following I would try everything possible to suppress my female tendencies. I could go for many months without being female, although I didn't make a rational decision to do this, and looking back on things now, it was almost a subconscious thing. But after a few months I would get the urge to dress up and for the next few years that was the routine. I would be male for many months and then Julie would reappear.

As a male I was quite controlled and organized, both in my career and socially. In contrast, my female periods were more frantic and disorganized. When I felt I had to be female, I had to do it immediately and nothing else mattered. A phase like this would last for around three months and then would stop as abruptly as it started and I would just slip back into the flow of what most people would say was a normal life, for as long as eight or nine months. It was, however, during those long periods of maleness that I made most of my errors and very bad decisions. Oddly, the outcome of some of those bad moves turned out to be quite positive in the medium and long term, although virtually everything I achieved in the 1980s and early 1990s would eventually be totally discarded as Julie evolved and took precedence once again. Ultimately, she would come to dominate forever.

In the early 1980s, though, during a big male period, I felt misguidedly determined to prove that I was 100% male – and what could be a more male occupation than being a fireman? The seeds of this idea were sown way back in the early 1960s; I remember Dad coming home with his fireman's uniform on and telling us tales of putting out big fires, and it really caught my imagination. As youngsters, me and my best friend Peter would often hang around outside the fire station gates in the hope that someone would be unfortunate enough to have a fire, and that we would see a fire engine come screaming out onto the busy street with siren blaring and lights flashing. Although we would hang around for ages we usually never got lucky, but as soon as we went away, it always seemed that a fire engine would speed past, and I would be absolutely thrilled when it turned out to be Dad driving it, and I would dream that some day I would be a fireman too. So it was really quite natural that I would eventually follow my dad into this admirable profession.

But although joining the fire service was very much influenced by the fact that Dad was a fireman – he still was when I joined – I also saw it very much as the thing to do if I was going to be male, and this choice really marked the start of my futile attempts to avoid what would turn out to be my inevitable path towards womanhood.

I didn't get into the fire brigade on my first attempt – in fact, it was only on my third attempt that I was successful, and even then it was because someone else who had been accepted had pulled out shortly after. I got a phone call one evening from the recruitment officer, who said that the other candidate had decided the job wasn't for him after all. I was next on the list and the job was mine if I still wanted it. I was caught off guard as the call came so unexpectedly, out of office hours. I must have hesitated because the officer then said, 'Well, do you still want it?' However, I was ready for him this time and excitedly said, 'Yes, I do!' He said I would get a letter in the post to confirm everything, along with instructions on what would happen next.

I knew the training would be hard, and the first step was to pass a medical to make sure I was fit enough for the job. It was the most comprehensive examination you could imagine, but I knew I was fit, and the only worry I had was whether I would be tall enough. At that time you had to be five feet six inches tall, and I knew it would be touch and go. When I was measured by the Brigade Doctor I thought it was no go when he said that I only measured five feet five and three quarters tall. The disappointment on my face must have been obvious, because he looked at me, said,

'Straighten your back a wee bit, sonny', and measured me again. Then he said, 'Sorry, my mistake – five feet six. Congratulations, that's you in.' But I really was just five feet five and three quarters.

From the word go it was all hard physical training, almost military-like. We had to run around the training ground with the officers shouting at us, very much like sergeant majors in the army, and we were continually running out hoses and rolling them up again, doing this over and over again; pitching ladders against the training tower, up and down, up and down till we got it right, in all kinds of weather and in the dark, as fires don't just happen in good weather during the day. It would be a long time before we actually saw a fire engine – let alone a fire – and the relentless physical training was gradually mixed with more and more theory in the classroom.

The general public generally doesn't appreciate how technical fire fighting is. It was back then in the early 1980s, and it's even more so nowadays; it's not just squirting water on the flames, although in years gone by the basic ethic of a firefighter was, first, to save life, second, to save property, and third, to offer humanitarian services. The classroom work started off investigating legal matters such as a firefighter's right to enter buildings. For example, if a building was adjacent to, or in front of one which was on fire, you could quite legally break into those buildings if it facilitated you reaching the burning building. We then moved on to theory about pump capacities, rope strengths, building structures, types of hazardous substances, breathing apparatus and much more. The lectures were endless and the training was never over – it continues throughout a firefighter's career as innovations in equipment and techniques are always coming along.

After basic training there is an assessment by the officers and those who make it through are deemed ready to go on the run – that is, they are ready for active service. Eventually I reached that stage and it wasn't long before my first fire call came. From then on my job really became a way of life. It was very exciting, but at the same time it carried a huge responsibility, and I was always very aware that people's lives could be in my hands.

I was definitely in the middle of a big male phase at this point, and I really thought that firefighting would quell any female tendencies. However, I was once again working in a totally male-dominated environment, with all the usual bravado from the lads in the fire station. I knew from past experience that if they ever found out about the way I was, my life would be hell and this is exactly what happened some years later. But even back then there was one person on the same fire crew as me who already knew all the deep secrets from my past. That person was my dad. At that time though, I'm pretty sure he also thought I had firmly left my troubled past behind me.

It was quite uncommon, but not unheard of, for a father and son to be on the same crew, though we were rarely paired up together on the same hose crew or breathing apparatus team – possibly so that in the event anything went wrong, two members of the same family wouldn't be put in harm's way at the same time. But we did attend the same callouts together – only for a couple of years after I joined. In 1985 Dad retired after serving a record-breaking thirty years in the fire service.

Another record had also been broken – since joining the fire service I had gone for almost a whole year without feeling the urge to dress up as a female. It did cross my mind occasionally, but that's as far as it went. I would say to myself, 'You're in the fire service now, so you can't be doing that sort of thing.' But it would only take a single event to trigger my female side back into action.

That event happened when I was playing a gig with the band in a big club in Camelon in Falkirk. It was a very busy night, and from my elevated position on stage I had noticed a table with four women round it, all having a great time. Something struck a chord with me and I couldn't stop looking at them. During the break, on my way to the bar, I had to walk past their table and I glanced over at them again.

One of them said to me, 'Do you have a problem, mate?'

I immediately replied, 'No, not at all', and then, to show them that I knew their secret, I said in my best female voice, 'It takes one to know one.'

That broke the ice and they immediately struck up a conversation with me. We all compared notes, so to speak, and had a drink together, but I soon had to go back on stage. We hadn't exchanged numbers and our paths never crossed again. But the encounter provided me with more confirmation that I wasn't alone in the world.

Although I was determined that this encounter wouldn't affect me, within a week, and after almost one year, Julie was back again, this time with a vengeance. Her influence was stronger than ever and for the next few months she was all that mattered. Even when we were speeding along the road in the fire engine, being Julie was all I could think about. I have to say though, when we got to the incident, whether it was a fire, a road accident or just something minor like a cat stuck up a tree, I was totally focused on the job in hand. Quite rightly, my comrades expected me to give 100% in any situation, whether it was serious or just routine, and I in turn expected them to give the same; our very survival could depend on this trust. For me, this camaraderie is one of the most powerful elements of any firefighting team; I knew it then and I know it now. However, this trust between my comrades and myself would be tested to the very limit in just a few years' time.

I truly loved being in the fire brigade It was one of the most exciting, challenging and rewarding experiences I ever had, and I was totally dedicated to the job. I was determined to be successful, but being Julie wasn't conducive to that. So although Julie had recently dominated, I quite consciously decided that she had to be out of my life and I was going to be him instead of her.

Other aspects of my life were going very well too – the band was becoming more and more successful, and financially things were very healthy indeed. At the same time my relationship with Anne was going from strength to strength and we had recently bought a flat together in Callander. I remember going to the solicitor's office in Stirling to sign the final papers; the Madness single Our House was in the charts and we sang it all the way back in the car. It seemed so appropriate at the time.

Although everything was going so well and I really wanted to live a male life, I was continually drawn back to thoughts of Julie, and I'm sure Anne knew what was going through my mind. But to her credit, she seemed to tolerate it – as I said before, she must have loved me so much, just as I loved her. So on the 16th of April 1983 we got married. I didn't do it to prove I was male, I did it because I genuinely loved Anne for all the right reasons at the time. But, selfishly, I still always had my bit on the side –yours truly, Julie.

When I'd told Mum, some months earlier, that Anne and I were getting married she didn't seem too happy about it and I thought that maybe she didn't like Anne very much. Not much was said at the time, which was always the way it was in our family – we just didn't talk about things. A few weeks later I asked Mum, 'Are you not too happy about Anne and me getting married? Her reply was, 'Of course I'm not happy about it – what in God's name is Anne thinking? Does she not know what she's getting herself into?'

I instantly realized that I was looking at the situation in completely the wrong way. Mum was trying to protect Anne, not me. That was the first time that Mum had come down off the fence and openly made her feelings known to me. Up until then it had just been a remark here or there, or a disapproving look, or she just wouldn't talk to me for days or weeks on end. But to this day I don't know if she ever discussed our marriage with Anne; if they did talk about it, they never told me.

However, when it came to the wedding, both Mum and Dad were there, as were my brother and two sisters, all of whom knew my secrets. I think they probably thought that marriage – or, more likely, Anne – would sort me out. I think they needed some hope, something to cling on to and as far as they were concerned this just might be the one thing that would change me, as they had all come to know Anne was a very intelligent, strong-willed, capable and extremely popular woman.

After that incident with Mum, we never really openly broached the subject of my other life again as it was too painful for both of us – especially for Mum. Even in the early 1980s this type of issue still wasn't something that was openly talked about. But there was never any question of her disowning me or anything like that – she loved me then and she still does today, and I love her dearly and always will – she's my mum.

I was beginning to realize why certain things had happened in the past within our family. I'm not saying that I was deliberately left out of things, but if I had a project on the go I was generally left to get on with it myself. For instance, when I bought my first set of drums at the age of fourteen I was given no encouragement whatsoever, and the idea was dismissed as a passing phase and a waste of money. Likewise, at fifteen, I built a pigeon loft completely on my own after carrying every piece of timber, plank by plank, half a mile from the timber merchant's to get it home. This lack of encouragement from my parents had always been the case since an early age. But it meant I learned how to go it alone, and that and my growing determination would help me achieve my goals in the years to come.

Being left out of things actually started way back at primary school. If there was a sports team to be picked I would invariably be left standing on my own, embarrassed and sad, as no one ever wanted me on their team. Sadly, this is a scenario that has followed me through life and it even continues to a certain extent to this day, although in a more subtle way and in different circumstances.

After getting married in 1983 I really thought I could have my cake and eat it and the battle between my male and female side was in full swing again. But I was in the fire brigade and I was married to a woman – what could be more male than that? So my male side was again winning for now – at least most of the time – and Anne seemed to put up with my short periods of going off the rails. She may even have thought that I would eventually stop needing to be Julie altogether. But there was one thing that had niggled away at me for years – ever since I had heard the word 'transvestite' mentioned in that Michel Caine movie. The dictionary definition was: 'A person who wears clothes normally worn by the opposite sex'. Yes, that was me – but it continued '(for sexual gratification)'. That was not me, no, not at all.

Now I was starting to look for some other answer, if indeed there was one. I didn't mix with others like me by going to places in the cities where they congregated, because at the time I just saw them as a crowd of queens and that just wasn't my scene. I didn't, and don't, mean any disrespect to them – I knew what every one of them was going through, and my use of the word 'queens' was wrong, but that's the way I saw it at the time. I preferred to go into straight bars – all I wanted to do was fit in and be seen as a normal female on the street. As I just wasn't in the know about these things, I was becoming more uncomfortable with the label 'transvestite', but at that time it was the only name I had heard that related in any way to someone who felt like me. Then, just when I was least expecting it, I happened to see an item on News at Ten where someone was complaining about the NHS paying for 'transsexuals' to have sex-change operations.

Well, this was another bolt from the blue. It was the first time I had ever heard the word 'transsexual', and just as I had done when I first heard the word 'transvestite', I rushed over to the dictionary and read the following definition: A person who is born belonging anatomically to one sex but who feels him or herself to be or desires to become a member of the opposite sex.

This revelation absolutely floored me. Had I finally found out once and for all what I actually was? This definition seemed to fit me, in my own mind at least. Since I had been seven years old I had felt more at ease watching other girls and wishing I could be one. In my teenage years I had loved dressing up, but there was never anything sexual about it. I just felt it was right for me. Then, through my twenties, I just wanted to be seen as an ordinary female – out shopping or in selected bars, but not gay bars – I didn't like them then and don't like them now. So was I a transsexual? Well, yes, at the time I thought that this was the answer. However, it would be another twenty years before I would finally find out once and for all what I had been struggling with since the age of seven.

Even though I had this new label 'transsexual', which I definitely felt more comfortable with than 'transvestite', my male side still wasn't anywhere nearly ready to accept the definition – even when the very same word was suggested to me by one of Anne's friends who knew me well and who, unbeknown to me, had come to this same conclusion about me some years previously.

As time went on I began to wish that I could confide in someone and this need grew quickly and intensely. I was in a situation where, on the one hand, I was desperate to conceal my female tendencies, and on the other hand I was racking my brains to come up with someone I could tell about everything, because I needed some way of lifting the weight off my shoulders. But I had to be sure that whoever I selected would be discreet. At times this need to find a confidante would completely consume all of my thoughts. It was just another twist in the conflict between my male and female sides.

I decided that whoever this person turned out to be, they definitely had to be female, as I felt I could talk to women more easily and I felt a woman would be more understanding. I also saw myself as one of them anyway.

During this quest I struck up a friendship with a lady called Sheila Bidwell, who had asked me to do some work for her. As well as playing in the band and being in the fire brigade I was also running a small, one-person general maintenance business, doing all sorts of things from joinery to window cleaning and landscaping – just about anything really. I got a call from Sheila one day; she lived just down the road from my mum and dad on the outskirts of Callander and wanted me to cut down some hedges and build a ranch fence in their place. She was so pleased with my work that she offered me more – she wanted a new kitchen fitted and various other things done. While I was working there, Sheila and I got on really well and I found it really easy to talk to her. Some days I think we spent more time chatting and having coffee and biscuits than working. She had a very positive attitude to life; she had had a successful heart operation and it was her positivity that really began to inspire me not to look on the dark side, and not to dwell on the past.

'The only thing that is important now is your future,' she said, and that attitude is something I have in copious amounts to this day, thanks partly to Sheila. Anyway back then, I had become so friendly with Sheila that I was now confident that, if I told her about Julie, I was sure that she would be okay about it. I just needed the right opportunity to tell her.

We were having one of our extended coffee breaks one morning and I was building up to coming out with it during one of our great putting-the-world-to-rights conversations when she suddenly said to me, 'Right, is there anything you want to tell me?'

I said, 'What do you mean?' She had caught me totally on the hop; somehow she had beaten me to it and I just didn't know what to say.

She said that her son Glen had told her he had heard that I was a bit dodgy and that I was a cross-dresser. That's the way some people described someone like me, struggling with gender issues. If they didn't understand it or didn't want to understand it, you were labelled as being dodgy, or worse. Glen's source got two things wrong, though. I wasn't a cross-dresser and I wasn't dodgy. Sheila told me that she already knew about me, and she was wondering if I was ever going to tell her, given that we had become such good friends. When I asked her how she knew, she said it was four things initially.

'When you were stretching up to cut the branches off the hedge your buttocks looked like those of a woman; secondly, when you sat with your legs crossed during coffee time your top knee was pointing upwards and your hands were clasped round it with your foot pointing outwards – men don't sit like that; thirdly, talking to you is just like talking to a woman and that's why I feel so comfortable with you. And, oh yes, your hands are certainly not workman's hands – they're far too slim, they're women's hands.'

Well, that completely blew me away because it took me back twenty-one years to when I was seven years old in primary school and my childhood schoolfriend Alison had said to me in art class, 'You have small hands – they are girls' hands.'

I became very emotional and began to cry and Sheila asked me what was wrong. I told her about what Alison had said all those years ago in primary school, and about how I hadn't known at the time why I was so happy about the fact that I had girls' hands.

Around the time I was having this conversation with Sheila, I was also planning to return to the place that had made me so happy in my youth – the Isle of Coll. For me it would be an emotional return after an absence of fifteen years.

Since Anne and I had got together we had been on a fair few holidays to all the usual places – package holidays in Spain and the like – and by 1984 we were becoming a bit bored with them. We had been to Lloret de Mar that year, and when we got back home I said to Anne, 'Do you fancy a change next year?' I was thinking of our family holidays to the Isle of Coll, way back in the 60s. I had mentioned the island to her from time to time and she was warming to the idea, so we thought we might try it.

I remembered that, as a youngster, when I was on Coll it seemed to take my mind off my female tendencies, and I was hoping the island might still have this effect on me, even after all those years. Of course, I also had fond memories of our family holidays there, and the Isle of Coll had always drifted in and out of my thoughts over the years.

Hard to believe, but Coll shared some similarities with the Spanish resorts Anne and I had been visiting. It had the sun, as Coll and the neighbouring island of Tiree regularly have the highest number of hours of sunshine recorded in the UK, and it certainly had the beaches; but the similarity ends there. The difference between the beaches on the Isle of Coll and the beaches in Spain couldn't be more stark. Where the latter have thousands of people on them, those on Coll literally have no one on them.

Given my fifteen-year absence, and before I returned to the island, I wondered if it might have changed. Fortunately I was pleasantly surprised; the most noticeable change, for the better, was that the island now had mains electricity.

No electricity had definitely been a novelty for my family when we came on holiday there, way back in the sixties. I remember the house being very quiet as there were no radios, televisions or anything like that playing. There were televisions, but the islanders had a very novel way of watching them – they used to park the farm tractor outside the living-room window and use it as a kind of generator, hooking up their television sets to the battery. This produced a very poor-quality picture, and I'm not sure about the sound either, because the tractor was noisily revving its head off outside the window. But to us kids the novelty factor was great. Once the TV was switched off the whole house would fall silent, apart from people's voices. The lights were all gas mantles in the middle of the ceiling; you had to turn on the gas and stand on a chair to light them with a match. When they were lit I thought they sounded like small jet engines.

I knew it would be inevitable that some things would have changed on the island, but I hoped that it would still hold the same magic for me and bring me the same feelings of peace and happiness as it had done many years ago.

chapter five

dark days, big revelations, big trouble

When I returned to the Isle of Coll after all those years it wasn't long before I was re-discovering all the secret places of my childhood. Unlike the package holidays to Spain, my love for the island was as strong as ever, and indeed Anne would also come to love the place in just a matter of days, and it would become our regular destination for the next few years.

On that first holiday with Anne on Coll I immediately felt the weight of my gender issues lifting. For some reason, one I have never been able to explain, I felt comfortable within myself on Coll. I had always felt this way. I also found that the people on Coll whom I remembered from my childhood were as welcoming as ever. They had no knowledge of the problems I was facing in my day-to-day life and for that reason it was easy to recapture the innocence and carefree days of my previous holidays there.

We would eventually move to Coll in 1995, but only after a turbulent decade, mostly caused by the increasingly troublesome predicament that I found myself in, relating to my ongoing gender issues. I say 'predicament' because that was exactly what my confusion was. It was becoming more and more evident that I had to do something about my situation. I hadn't a clue about where it was taking me or how it might end – or even if it would ever end. Would I continue on what seemed like a road to hell? But it was the worry that I might never find my true self that terrified me and that would almost drive me to total destruction.

After years of battling with myself and trying to suppress my female side I was beginning to ask myself more and more questions and the one that kept returning was why? Why was I like this? I have always known that I certainly didn't ask to be like this, and it certainly isn't my parents' fault. And as far as I know no one else in our family, past or present, has had similar issues.

Mum once said to me, on one of the few occasions when we did talk honestly and openly about me, that she thought she and Dad must have done something wrong, and she seemed so sad when she said this. That really upset me, and it was at that point that I realized it wasn't just me who was hurting or who didn't have any answers – we were all in the same predicament. I couldn't find a way to escape, and my family didn't know how to help me. Like me, they too had no one to turn to and had no answers for what was still almost a taboo subject. That is something that haunts me to this day. It was difficult enough for me to cope with so what must have it been like for my mum and dad?

The mid 80s was one of the lowest and darkest points of my journey. I even thought of ending it all as it seemed to be the only way to escape the turmoil within my body. But thankfully my resilience and willpower pulled me back from the brink time and time again.

My gender issues had grown and developed as I got older. As

I became more sophisticated, so did my female side. This meant that my understanding of my self became slightly clearer at every stage too. My carefree attitude, or the way I just accepted that this was the way life was going to be, was succumbing to the more mature me, who was starting to analyze and question my situation more and more as time went on. Because of this, my long-standing gender issues were fast evolving into a gender crisis, and the massive highs and lows were becoming more extreme and more frequent.

As far as Anne was concerned, I was taking liberties – I simply thought I could do what I liked without giving much thought to what she wanted, or what she was really feeling. I misguidedly assumed that she would always just accept and go along with what I was doing. I thought nothing about disappearing out dressed as Julie if I was given an opportunity to do so. Anne could pop to the shops and come back to find me gone with no note or anything to let her know where I was. She would be in no doubt as to what I was up to, but I never considered her feelings at all. The confusing thing was that this just wasn't me – I had loathed the way the men who I had worked with over the years had treated their wives, and yet here I was behaving in the same way. Even though it was for a totally different reason, it just proved yet again that when my female side was in charge nothing else mattered, and I felt powerless to do anything about it.

The tide was very slowly starting to turn away from the predominantly male phase I had gone through in the early eighties, in favour of my female side again. As my life as Julie evolved I became her, even in my dreams. This was something new and seemed to develop apace as Julie became more sophisticated. Was this wishful thinking, was my mind just being what it naturally wanted to be, or were my dreams telling me the direction I should be taking? Each possibility seemed very plausible and wondering about this occupied my thoughts continually.

At this time I was constantly crying and very emotional, especially when I went to bed at night. I used to think, wouldn't it be great if I could wake up in the morning and every thing was fixed and I was Julie? I had this thought pretty well every night for the next few years. These thoughts would eventually develop into something much more difficult to deal with and would once again almost push me to the very brink. The twenty-first century would sweep in before I got to total breaking point, though, and at that point I was forced to give in to what was always inevitable.

There were a few good and positive things happening, or about to happen, as well, but sadly these would be overtaken by less fortunate events, all of them created by me, and me alone. I was heading for very dark days indeed, would be forced to make a huge and final effort to turn away from everything that my body and mind was screaming at me. As usual, I felt I had to try and do what was expected of me, and what others thought I should be doing, instead of listening to my own body and mind. It was this peer pressure that confused me and prolonged my agony.

Our trips to the Isle of Coll were becoming much more frequent and we felt the place was doing us good. It certainly took my mind off some of the issues that had plagued me back home in Callander. My ongoing battle to suppress Julie and the growing suspicions of everyone who knew me was lying even more heavily on my shoulders. Again, Coll seemed to relieve that pressure and

Anne too, was becoming much more at home, there on the island. But every time we returned home after our holiday we would be completely depressed; not just because we didn't want to go back to work, but because Coll was exerting its influence on us. It's that sort of place; it seems to draw you in. It's very quiet, and back in the 1980s it was still a million miles away from the hustle and bustle of the mainland.

However, once we'd been back home for a couple of weeks we were back into the usual business of getting on with life, and had to be content with knowing that next year's holiday would eventually come round again.

In 1987 getting back to business really meant just that and within a few weeks Julie was also back, her influence growing stronger with every month that passed, and it was this that was gradually eroding Anne's tolerance of the situation. In the past she reluctantly accepted Julie, knowing full well what I was doing, but maintaining an 'out of sight, out of mind' attitude. Whether this was down to her love for me or because she just wanted a quiet life or because it was just convenient, I don't know. We never actually discussed what Anne really felt and wanted and I took her silence as a tacit acceptance of my behaviour, whether that was really the case or not.

We were both doing very well in our careers at the time and were also doing well financially, so maybe she just didn't want to rock the boat. However, the cracks were starting to appear, and the situation where I was getting the best of both worlds could never last. Anne was becoming more and more unhappy with the way I was, and with the fact that I was just taking it for granted that she would put up with the way I lived forever. We began to have blazing rows where she would resort to threatening to spill the beans if I didn't stop doing what I was doing. When this happened I would go on the straight and narrow for a while, but eventually I would just slip back into my old ways and we would go through the whole process again. It wasn't that Anne had suddenly become fed up with Julie but more the fact that I was constantly eroding her trust and continuing to ignore how she felt. This cycle recurred more and more, in different degrees of intensity and with many variations in its outcome and it was becoming blindingly obvious to me was that I definitely wasn't going to get away with this lifestyle for ever.

'Getting away with it' is actually the wrong term to use, because I wasn't trying to get away with anything, though that's how it must have looked, and this was something else that I was just beginning to realize. In fact, this was how I was born and I was simply doing what my mind was telling me to do. The only thing forcing me to try and hide Julie at all costs was the knowledge that I wouldn't be accepted by the general public, and I feared being ridiculed by those who weren't prepared to even try and understand who I was. In years to come, the people who found what I was doing the hardest to accept were those who I thought would be the ones who were best equipped to handle it – people who had travelled widely and reckoned they were wise to the ways of the world; these were professional business people who lived in a material world and disliked people who didn't conform to what they perceived as normality; even my GP who, like many others in the 1980s, didn't know what to do or say when faced with my situation.

Anne went to that same doctor once with a routine ailment and after she had been treated for it the GP asked her if there was anything else she wanted to discuss. She replied that there was, and told him she was a bit fed up about what I was doing. When she explained what that was, thinking he would offer some support or advice, he immediately said to her, 'Is he into young boys?'

Anne said, 'No, certainly not, he just wants to be a woman', to which the doctor said, 'Well, there's nothing I can do about it.' And that was that, end of. At the time I thought this was an outrageous question to ask her and I still do.

Even although Anne was becoming more intolerant of what I was doing, she was very upset about the doctor's lack of understanding and she told me about it as soon as she got home. At first I was extremely angry, not just because my feelings were hurt – but because Anne was hurt too. She had hoped to be given some support or advice and she was given nothing, due to sheer ignorance or unwillingness on the part of our doctor to tackle the subject. I was facing an uphill battle, a situation that would exist to a certain degree for many more years.

What upset me most at the time was wondering what everyone else would think if they knew about me. If doctors could make wildly wrong assumptions about people like me then what hope did I have with ordinary people in my community? I also realised for the first time, after the doctor's dismissive treatment of Anne, that those close to me could also be unfairly treated by association. I felt utterly powerless when even people in positions of authority had no insight into ,or inclination to explore, these types of issues.

As my gender battle intensified, my female side, Julie, was becoming ever stronger, and I was becoming increasingly confident as a woman. I was now even venturing out onto my home town high street as Julie. Callander was a very busy tourist destination then, and still is, so there were literally thousands of people there from all over the country. It was quite easy just to mingle in the busy street or in any of the many big shops, and if I saw someone I knew I would just turn my head and walk past them. As far as I know I got away with it totally unrecognized, and this really gave me great confidence. However, I only ever walked around my home town in this way when Anne was at work. Our unspoken understanding was that if she didn't know about it then it didn't bother her – up to a point. This situation was, by then, wearing a bit thin, and the daft thing was that she always knew when I had been out as Julie anyway.

But it would be one of these 'Julie trips' to the city that would completely change my life for ever, and all the problems that I had had up until then would pale into insignificance in comparison to what I would soon face.

The wild swings between my male and female sides were becoming much more intense, and this was very difficult to control. My struggle to contain Julie was becoming quite destructive to my wellbeing, in every aspect of my life. Try to imagine going to bed each night wishing for a miracle to transform you into the opposite gender by morning – this is what I would do every single night. But of course I would wake up and nothing had changed. The toughest aspect to deal with was knowing that I had to get through yet another day of sheer hell as a man. I would have my breakfast and go to work; on the way I would go into the newsagent's to buy my newspaper and see a smartly dressed female, and my mind would completely turn full circle. I would stare at this person, not because I desired her, but because I desperately wanted to be like her.

So my life was changing. The old cycle of being a few weeks

male and a few weeks female was becoming a crazy, frenzied swing between feeling male or female depending on what I was confronted with at any point throughout the day. This caused me to almost spiral out of control on a daily basis. I'm not sure how I got through those days, let alone how I performed my duties as a firefighter, given that I could be called out at a moment's notice and have to give 100%. On a shout I had to devote my mind to the job in hand; no question about it and no margin for error, as the lives of the public and my colleagues, as well as my own life, could depend on it. But when the call came I was always able to focus my mind on the job and no one could have imagined in a million years what was going through my mind, day in, day out.

Exactly the same thing happened when I played in the band. I would be completely focused on the job when we left for a gig – although, unlike my job in the fire service, lives were not at stake. However, it was still of the utmost importance that I performed exactly as required, not just for my fellow band members, but for the satisfaction of the people who had paid good money to come and hear us play.

Venues were, of course, full of women dressed up for a night out, and the sight of them would, in an instant, transport me to a place where all I could think of was that I wanted to be just like them. So it took a huge amount of concentration to focus on my drumming, which held the whole band together. If I faltered and messed up the whole band messed up, and I just had to find the willpower to keep my mind on the music, at least for the duration of each number.

In terms of my gender I was definitely in a state of limbo again. My dilemma still wasn't the sort of thing I could discuss with anyone – not even my doctor, as had been demonstrated by his ignorant treatment of Anne, some time earlier. Those strange-sounding names – 'transvestite' and 'transsexual' – were all I had to go on. Although 'transsexual' seemed to fit my profile better, this wasn't quite the whole story, and a full diagnosis wouldn't be made for another fifteen years. A lot of very troubled water would have to flow under the bridge before that.

One of the main reasons I wasn't gaining any information or knowledge about what I was really 'suffering' from was that I couldn't, or wouldn't, face up to what was troubling me. Crucially, I felt I couldn't talk to anyone about this. I couldn't even ask the very person that one would think could, and should, help – my ignorant and downright unhelpful doctor. I don't suppose this was completely intentional on his part. I now think to some degree that what happened to myself and Anne highlights the sheer lack of training about, or understanding of, what was still at that time a taboo subject.

The other reason I wasn't gaining any knowledge on the subject was that I had never really mixed with others like me. There were a few reasons why I didn't see myself as 'one of them', but the one in particular which rather confused me at the time was that the majority of other transsexuals whom I had met, or knew about, were still all sexually attracted to women, which I just couldn't understand. Even when my male side was more dominant, I had never been attracted to women in that way. I had fancied men from a young age, although I didn't see myself as gay. This may sound strange, but I had always thought of myself as being a heterosexual female whereas the majority of transsexuals I did know identified themselves as lesbians. Also, while many socialised together and inevitably drew attention to themselves, purely because of who they were, I preferred doing what I was more comfortable with which was just trying to fit in and not be labelled as one of that social group. I suppose this attitude made me a bit of a loner in the female side of my double life.

The 1980s were coming to an end, and it had been a decade of great turbulence in every aspect of my personal life – so much so that the difficulties I experienced had become almost routine, even if they were unbelievably complicated and erratic, to say the least. I had struggled, sometimes on a daily basis, attempting to suppress the female side of my personality, causing myself great personal anguish and, I'm sure, creating the same anguish for Anne.

Any routine or normality I had was about to be shattered by one single event that I could not have foreseen. It was a simple case of me being in the wrong place at the wrong time. I suppose it was inevitable, but it is quite incredible that what finally took place hadn't happened much earlier. This particular event triggered what would result in one of the biggest changes to my life so far. For the first time in my entire life, my gender dilemma provoked a hostile reaction and even the threat of violence towards me – albeit from a tiny minority of people.

It happened during one of my outings to the city as Julie. These were usually when Anne was on the night shift in her job at a residential home run by the Church of Scotland, as this gave me the perfect opportunity to do as I wished. My plan was that when she got back from work in the morning I would already be back home and tucked up safely in bed.

It was a Sunday night – the night I would usually meet my

friend Sue in Edinburgh. I had left the house in a rush for some reason and hadn't quite finished doing my makeup, so I thought I would stop on the way and do it somewhere quiet before driving to Edinburgh. My route took me through the town of Bridge of Allan, where I found a quiet residential street and parked under a street light to finish doing my makeup, aided by the car's interior light. This took me about ten minutes, but as I was putting my stuff back in my handbag I noticed that a car had pulled up about a hundred yards behind me. No one got out of it, which at first puzzled me. Then I began to worry as I thought that someone was watching me, and all sorts of scenarios began to go through my mind. I started the car up and drove off, at which point the car behind started to follow me. This really worried me and I began to feel very scared.

All of a sudden blue flashing lights shone brightly in my mirrors. It was obviously a police car and knowing that, I felt quite relieved. That said, my relief rapidly turned to sheer terror when the police car pulled me over. I had never before felt such anxiety and I frantically tried to work out what I was going to say as they approached my car window. As I wound the window down, one of the officers said, 'Oh, good evening, madam.'

At that point I instantly knew I shouldn't lie to them, so I said, 'Sorry, Officer, this isn't what you think', because that's the only thing I could think to say at the time. The officer closest to me turned to his mate and said, 'Oh, no luck here, it's just a tranny.' Although I was extremely nervous, having no idea what was going to happen to me, at the same time I had a strange feeling of relief and an underlying sense that I was probably not going to be able to hide my lifelong secret any more. It felt strangely good.

This all happened in less than two minutes, but I was questioned for another half an hour. At first the police said I had only been stopped because there had been some break-ins around the area in the last few weeks, and because I was parked outside a big house it looked like I could have been casing it, just sitting in my car as I was. The comment about me only being a tranny was because they had been hoping to catch a burglar. They then moved on to the fact that I was dressed as, looked like and spoke like a woman. I explained the reason for this to them and they said I would have to come to the police station so that they could verify who I was – although they had already asked my name and checked my driving licence.

However, what I didn't realize at the time because I couldn't quite see their faces under the glow of the streetlamp, was that one of the policemen had been at school with me, I immediately recognized him when we got into the well-lit police office.

I said, 'Oh, it's you', and he said, 'Yes, but you've changed a bit, haven't you? How are you doing?'

The other guy said, 'You're better looking than my wife', and at this point I thought things were going better than I had envisaged. My old schoolmate and I proceeded to have a conversation about people we both knew from our school days. Eventually one of them said, 'Well, you've done nothing wrong – you can be on your way.' I thanked them and asked, 'Is this the end of it? Is my secret out then?' My former schoolmate said, 'There's nothing written down police-wise about the matter, as you've done nothing wrong.' But I think deep down I knew that things would be different from then on.

As I was about to leave, my old schoolmate said, 'If you need to stop and do yourself up in future, do it somewhere out in the country where no one will see you.' He seemed to be saying that what I chose to do was nothing to do with them.

I decided to carry on with my trip to Edinburgh, thinking that if my secret was out it wouldn't make any difference what I did that night. It wasn't until the drive home that it really started to sink in what had actually happened and I realized that it was very likely I had finally been found out, once and for all. Up until now only a very few people in my home town of Callander had an inkling about what I was up to and remarkably, up until then, none of them had ever said anything to anyone as far as I know. My friend Sheila was the only other person to know the truth about me, although perhaps three or four others suspected, even if they didn't really know the full extent of how I lived my life.

I was now facing the real prospect that my lifelong secret had been uncovered, as I was sure that the police officers in Bridge of Allan would be in touch with their colleagues in Callander, only a few miles up the road.   If this happened it was inevitable that there would be a backlash, not only for me but also for Anne. Yet again it would be me, and me alone, who would bring her heartache and turmoil, and this is one of the things from my past that I truly regret to this day.

Although I felt some sense of relief that my secret was probably out, at the same time the prospect terrified me. I had no idea what might lie ahead and in the following days I began to suffer from severe anxiety. I couldn't eat or sleep properly, and the worst thing was trying to go to work and go about my daily business as though nothing had changed. I had no idea who knew about me and who didn't. I became extremely paranoid about that, but the one thing that really puzzled me was why no one had mentioned anything.

After about a week I began to think I might have got away with it. Surely if the officers were going to say anything they would have done so by now? In some ways this state of limbo was worse than discovering that everyone now knew my secret. I remember wondering how I'd be able to carry on if the suspense continued much longer. Another two weeks went past and this feeling of just not knowing whether my secret was out or not was getting much worse. But there was one thing that my complicated and demanding life had taught me and that was never to let anything get me down, never let anything beat me, and never, ever, give up.

In some ways the treatment that had been meted out to me since my early schooldays had made me like this. I had gradually built up resistance to being put down all of the time by those who I mistakenly thought would help and try to understand me. That resistance and determination was something that I would need in huge quantities within weeks, if I was going to get through what would be the most difficult and dark days of my adult life so far.

As it happened it was about three weeks before anything was said following my encounter with the police in Bridge of Allan. The reason being that the police officer in Callander they had informed that night was my best mate's father, a mate who served on the same fire crew as me and so they sat on the information for a couple of weeks, trying to decide what to do about it. Eventually my mate's dad felt it was time to say something to his colleagues, and I don't hold that against him in any way.

Once the news was out, this huge revelation about me spread like wildfire. I was a member of the emergency services and we all worked very closely together. Although it was bad for me, and about to get much worse, it was also hard for others, especially so for my colleagues in the fire service. Each of them had their own way of dealing with the information. Some were indifferent or just accepted it, some found it difficult to comprehend, and some found it very difficult to comprehend. A minority couldn't or wouldn't accept it and probably would never do so.

Over the years I had got used to dealing with the problems and complications brought on by my gender issues. I had become quite adept at talking my way out of difficult situations or making excuses to cover things up that didn't look quite right to others, and I got away with it most of the time. However, this time was different; I had been caught red-handed by the police and there was no talking my way out of this one. I had been found out, and it was the big story all over my home town and beyond. But it was also the end of my agonising three-week wait and that was a huge relief, even if I knew I was in for a very rough ride indeed.

The day the shit hit the fan I had turned up at the fire station as normal and we had all sorts of procedures to carry out; equipment checks and that sort of thing. While we were all going about our various tasks the officers were in the watch room, where the day-to-day administration was done and, more importantly, where the fire calls were received from the fire control centre in Falkirk. As usual with these things, I was the last to know what was going on. All of the lads had probably discussed me at length in my absence. They must have been shocked to the core be told that one of their own was the polar opposite of everything they stood for. They were firemen, after all, and they had just discovered that one of their close-knit family was doing something they couldn't comprehend.

I could only have been about fifteen minutes into my shift when I was called into the watch room. As soon as I walked in I could see by the look on the two officers' faces that something was going to happen, and I was pretty sure that I knew exactly what was coming. I had been expecting this moment, even hoping for it. The suspense of the past three weeks had brought me close to the point of collapse and I just couldn't handle the tension any longer. This was probably one of the most defining episodes in my long journey so far. I had now reached the point where my secret was out in the open and instead of hiding it I was now going to have to talk about it, knowing that absolutely everyone now knew all about me. People would speculate wildly and make inaccurate assumptions about me and it would be up to me to put them right.

As ours was a small fire station we were all very close. There was the Leading Fireman and the Sub-Officer, who was in charge; above them there was a Station Officer and above him the Assistant Divisional Officer. All of them would soon be involved in this sensitive and awkward situation, and as far as I know, Central Region Fire Brigade had never had to deal with a situation like mine before. In the coming months my dilemma would go all the way to the top brass of the fire service.

For now, though, I was questioned by the two men in the watch room. They were my immediate bosses, and they just happened to be brothers. I was quite close friends with them both so it was quite easy to talk to them. Basically they just asked me if what they had been told was true and I, of course, confirmed everything. We talked in some detail for a while and then the Sub said, 'How are you feeling?' I said that I was so relieved everything was now out in the open and I was glad that they had confronted me with it at last.

They were very understanding about the whole situation, and

both of them remained that way through the next two difficult years. However, talking to them had been the easy part. I now had to explain myself to the lads and I knew for sure that this wouldn't be as straightforward.

I was very relieved that my dad had retired from the service two years previously, so at least he was spared the embarrassment of everything that followed. Being questioned by the whole crew was one of the most nerve-racking things I had ever experienced. Unfortunately, the situation descended into something of a kangaroo court, and there would be many of those over the next few weeks. The most frequently asked question was, 'Are you homosexual?' That was an easy one to answer, as my response was a categorical 'No, definitely not.'

I was absolutely certain about this and that seemed to be good enough for the majority of my crewmates. However there was a small group – I christened them the hardliners – who were hell bent on getting rid of me at all cost. The sheer pressure of being treated like some sort of freak by people who just weren't willing to accept me was pushing me to the brink. But my old determination to fend off the enemy was starting to kick in once again and I was beginning to wonder why I should give in to this pressure. After all, I was just doing what my mind was telling me to do.

One or two of the hardliners were now openly calling for my resignation, but there was a real mixed bag of opinions; from total, partial or reasonable acceptance, right down to those who just wanted rid of me. Inevitably, the decision was taken out of their hands and the issue went to a much higher level, where some of the top brass were okay with it and some were not – the same old story. No one knew what a transvestite or a transsexual was and why would they? As far as I know the brigade had never before been confronted with this situation.

The fire brigade proposed that I see a sexual health psychologist at Stirling University. They hoped this would give them some sort of an answer or understanding and that they could then decide what to do about me. From my point of view it seemed like a good idea; I, too, hoped the psychologist would shed some light on what was going on, not just for them, but for me too – maybe I would learn something new about myself.

About two weeks after being 'outed' by my workmates, I attended the appointment where I told the consultant everything he needed to know. I spoke about my entire past, and the consultant then wrote a report on his findings. I received a copy of this, as did my GP and the brigade doctor. With my agreement the report was then given to my superior officers and, once again with my full agreement, shown to all the lads in the station which was embarrassing and highly humiliating for me.

An extract from the consultant psychologist's report reads as follows:

> *The gentleman has a long history of dressing up in female garb and my findings are that he is a well-balanced transvestite with no homosexual tendencies and I see no reason why this should stop him performing his duties as a fireman.*

Well, I was wrong when I thought I might learn something about myself. This report showed that even so-called experts were still not fully acquainted with the facts in this field, even in 1990.

Actually, the only part he got right was that I was not homosexual – the psychologist completely failed to consider that I might be transsexual. However, at the time I was grateful to have something written down, purely because I hoped that it might help others to better understand me.

Over the years it has been this lack of knowledge or understanding on the part of both professionals and the public that I have found one of the most frustrating things to deal with – not being able to find anyone who had any answers or suggestions that might help me. For me at least, it wouldn't be until around 2002 and attitudes slowly began to change for the better.

An incident that happened at the fire station is just one example of how people got it so wrong. One of our crew was also a hand potter; he made cups and teapots and other bits and pieces and someone had what they thought was the brilliant idea of asking him to make tea cups for everyone in the station, since tea and biscuits are something of an institution in any fire station. Each cup was to be unique, with the individual's nickname on their cup. Well, I was dreading to see what mine would be and sure enough it turned out to be completely inappropriate: AC/DC was a totally incorrect description of me and this was done even after they had all read the psychologist's report stating that I was a transvestite and not homosexual or bisexual. Regardless of what the report said, the lads had obviously decided that I must be playing both fields, hence the nickname AC/DC.

The next couple of years at the fire station were a constant battle as the hardliners never really gave up and I was threatened with violence on more than one occasion, as well as being subjected to a barrage of verbal abuse from a tiny minority. But the one thing that still bonded me to everyone there, even the hardliners, was our underlying and uncompromising allegiance to each other as firefighters. Our fundamental code was, and still is, total trust that your mates would be there for you in any life-or-death situation – situations which definitely did arise. Each and every one of us knew that without that trust we could not function as a highly professional, highly skilled and dedicated team. Despite everything personal that was going on between us, we still all had that total, uncompromising trust, and that at least is something that I carry in my heart to this day. And deep down I still don't hold anything against any of them, not even the hardliners. I understand that everyone was just doing what they thought was the right thing for themselves at the time – I know that I certainly was. So I hold absolutely no grudges whatsoever.

It was to the credit of all the lads in the station that, even if some were at odds with me, they never involved Anne in any of our internal arguments over my issues, and indeed, their wives and girlfriends continued to include her in social activities. As usual, it was the women who were more understanding with regard to the direction I was heading in, and some of the fire wives and girlfriends were quite sympathetic towards me. I know it even caused friction between some of them and their men at times, though I never wanted to come between anyone.

However, there was someone who was threatening to break up my relationship with Anne, and that was Julie. Anne was at the stage now where she wanted my dressing as a female to stop, and I had also assured the lads at the station that I had stopped doing this. I made the drastic decision to burn all of my female clothes which Anne thought was encouraging, although she was, at the same time, sceptical. She often said to me, 'It doesn't matter what you do, I'll always know what you're up to, I can read you like a book. I know you better than you know yourself.'

She was absolutely right. I don't think anyone will ever understand me the way she did and given what I put her through over the years, she is surely one of the strongest-minded people I have ever known. She tried, over many years, to give me the support I needed to try and sort myself out and her determination, tolerance and patience were incredible. I'm certain that if it hadn't been for her I wouldn't be the person I am today, even if neither of us intended things to turn out quite the way they did.

Anyway, I did burn all my female possessions in the back garden one night to show Anne that I was serious about changing. Within days I was regretting having done so and then spent a small fortune replacing everything, from clothes to makeup. Julie was in me, I couldn't shake her off, even though over the next ten years I would continue to attempt to escape her clutches.

One such attempt involved us making the bold decision to sell up and move away to start a new life elsewhere. My attempts to escape weren't all conscious decisions, they were just part of the natural push and pull between what I suppose you could call my dual gender status, but my female side was definitely gaining ground and momentum. For the first time ever I was starting to look at my body in a completely different way. I was beginning to say to myself, 'I think I've been born into the wrong body.' I know this sounds like a cliché now, but back in 1991 I had genuinely never heard of the concept before, although I really was beginning to feel that this was definitely the case with me. I had no idea if it was even possible to be born into the wrong body, but I was beginning to think that it might be the answer that had eluded me for the previous twenty eight years, since the age of seven when I realized that I was different from other boys.

From 1991 it would be another thirteen years before I would get a definitive answer to my dilemma, for now I would have to struggle on and my turmoil would only get worse, very much worse, before it would get better, as the highs and lows of my life continued through the nineties.

The reaction from the lads in the fire station was in stark contrast to that of the lads in the band. They were totally unfazed by the revelation that I was a transvestite (I'm using this name because that's what everyone now had me down as; although it was incorrect, it was just easier to let them think that). The lead singer even cheerfully announced to the audience at selected gigs that we had a cross-dressing drummer. This always got a chuckle from the crowd, and anything that encouraged them to interact with us was a good thing – though I did ask him not to do it in some of the tough working men's and miners' welfare clubs in central Scotland. He agreed to that of course, knowing that we would probably get booed off stage, or worse, in some of those places at the mention of the word transvestite.

Different attitudes in different situations in different places and in different walks of life are something I've encountered throughout most of my journey. As a result, I've learned over the years where it was and wasn't safe to go. For instance, I wouldn't have dreamed of going into a working men's pub on my own dressed as Julie, but I knew I would be all right going into a lounge bar where there were couples and groups of females.

This was knowledge gained the hard way, starting in my early days of going out as a female. It was a steep learning curve that began soon after I had passed my driving test in 1973, when I went from being confined to my home town of Callander to being able to spread my female wings and take to the bigger cities of central Scotland. I was now able to frequent a wide range of pubs and clubs and made the most of my new-found freedom. But just when I thought I'd got it all sorted, I found myself in a situation I simply couldn't have anticipated.

I had decided, just for a change, to go to Dundee. It was the first time I had ever been there so I didn't know my way around the venues and had no idea what to expect. I drove around for a while until I spotted a couple of suitable-looking pubs. I usually chose well-lit disco-type places with a bit of a buzz and noise, as it was easier to mingle with the crowd. Anyway, I decided on a pub that looked like the one for me and managed to get the car parked just around the corner. I was only 21 at the time and quite a hot-looking wee bird, so I just looked like the majority of other young females in there that night. I enjoyed mingling with people as Julie, having a couple of drinks, and was happy to be accepted as just another young girl in the bar. My night went well until it was time to leave.

Unfortunately the door to the lounge had been locked to stop any more people getting in because the place was jam-packed, and the only way out was through the well-guarded door of the adjoining public bar. This was something I just hadn't anticipated and unfortunately the public bar was my idea of the pub from hell. It was full of the very type of men I was always careful to avoid, but now I had to face of the prospect of fighting my way through a crowd of mostly drunk working men who had probably been drinking since finishing work at 5 o'clock. I decided I just had to go for it, but I had only got a few feet through when some men started to grope me as they shouted, 'Come on babe, get 'em off.' and much more besides. Worse than that was their wandering hands, accompanied by, 'Gie's a feel at your fanny! Come on, get yer tits oot!'

At this point I really felt I was in deep trouble. I was surrounded and there was so much noise in the pub that none of this could be seen or heard by the bar staff. I began to panic and my real worry was that these men would discover that I was not what they thought I was. I knew if they discovered that then their drunken fumbling would turn to anger and probably violence. Somehow, in the chaos of the crowd, I was miraculously carried towards the door and the look of terror on my face must have been clear. Out of the blue I was thrown a lifeline when one of the bouncers spotted me in the mayhem and immediately came to my rescue. He could see my distress and as a mass of bodies spilled out on to the street he offered to escort me back to my car where he stood by until I drove off.

That incident was a terrifying experience for me – I was totally traumatized by the knowledge that I could easily have been beaten up, or worse. It was certainly a lesson learnt and I realized that I hadn't done my homework properly on the place before I had gone in.

Most importantly, even then, I knew for sure that I was on a very dangerous journey indeed.

chapter six

an untenable position

Ever since the mid-1960s my holidays to the Isle of Coll had been a real tonic, an escape from my double-gender issues, and Anne and I had been going to the island together since 1985. Even in the 90s my troubles still seemed to disappear every time I set foot on Coll and Anne was also aware that I was much more relaxed when we were there. We both began to think that moving to Coll might just be the answer; the key to me shrugging off Julie for good. Looking back, I can see that even then, I really knew in my heart of hearts that I was a female inside. But sometimes people make choices and take decisions just to appease others, especially those close to us, and we end up going down a road that we know is probably the wrong one, but we do it anyway. Moving to the Isle of Coll with Anne was just one example of that in my life, and the next ten years would see me doing a lot more of the same in what would be a final push to escape what had always been inevitable.

The start of this phase in 1993 would see us buying a plot of land on Coll, the place I had loved since my childhood and the place Anne had grown to love over the past few years. Meanwhile though, back in Callander, everyone now knew about the double life I had been leading and I was having huge problems with some of the guys at the fire station. The only reason I was still there was that I had promised my workmates I had turned a new leaf. As far as they were concerned I had stopped 'dressing up' as they put it, and I was essentially the same as them again. But in truth I was slipping back into my old ways. My feelings weren't going to go away, not ever, and I now had the unbelievably difficult task of again living a double life, this time knowing that all the sceptics were watching my every move for signs that I was up to my old tricks again. And they were absolutely right. I was letting them down; I was letting all my friends down; I was letting my family down and, most of all, I was letting Anne down. She was the one person who had supported and believed in me over the years. I truly didn't want to let anyone down, but my female side was so overpowering that I didn't actually have much control over it.

I tried to persuade everyone my 'cross-dressing' was a thing of the past, but it was a futile effort, and anyway, as I would soon learn, there comes a point where no one really believes or trusts you any more. I'd known deep down for some time that the day would come when I would be forced out of the fire service. The hardliners were never going to leave me alone until they got their way, and their way was the high road for me. I had resisted the inevitable because I still felt I had a lot to offer; I knew I was a good firefighter, with years of experience. Of course, I knew I was different and that there were people against me as well as those who supported me, but I thought, 'Why should I leave? After all, I love what I do, and why should I go just because some people don't like me because of who I am?' I had done nothing wrong and being a transvestite certainly wasn't illegal, so there were no grounds for getting rid of me.

"DR. FINLAY'S CASEBOOK"

LOCAL CHILDREN FILMED

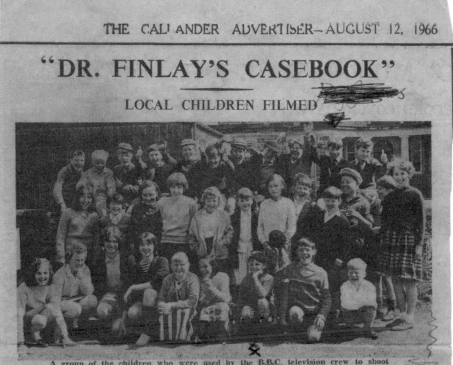

A group of the children who were used by the B.B.C. television crew to shoot playground scenes for a future "Dr Finlay's Casebook" story.

Recently, our columns carried a request from the BBC for children willing to take part in the filming of an episode in the saga of "Dr Finlay's Casebook." For over thirty local children this was the chance of a lifetime. Children, though they may not always know it, are natural actors since they are nearer to the world of pure imagination than are we world-weary adults. To act was a marvellous idea, but to act as school-children during the holidays could only be described as "super." Duly, the bairns reported to Tannochbrae school at 9 a.m. on Monday morning and quickly discovered that being an actor is not so glamorous as it looks. They found that much of an actor's life, on location at least, consists of waiting and of performing the same simple actions over and over again. Perhaps they discovered, the actions aren't so simple after all, perhaps there is more in this than meets the TV viewer's eye!

Finally came the Callander bairns' moment. They were to come rushing noisily out of school. So effective were they that their noise was audible a full quarter of a mile away!

On Tuesday, they were to play in the playground. Their enthusiasm, their inventiveness dismayed the professional actors a trifle when one young enthusiast "bopped" another over the head with his school bag.

Actors have traditionally a strong team sense. That this can infect a "part-timer" was plain to one parent when his daughter announced after her second day's work, with a happily nonchalant plural. "Oh we've some work to do tomorrow that we didn't finish today."

At last the children's moment of TV glory was over. They were full of pleasant memories of the television team's appreciation of their services. One young actress came home and announced proudly. "It's been great! I've had two dinners in the Bridgend Hotel, they gave me "this smashing box of sweets and I've earned my first pay!" and she flourished some paper money. "I'll spend it in Stirling," she added with that considering look on her face that all males recognise.

We understand from Miss Rees, the Assistant Producer, that the BBC team were very impressed by what she called the naturalness of the children. Indeed, Miss Rees, like many other BBC people we have been privileged to meet, sensed the essence of small town life, its easiness, its homeliness and its freedom from that curse of big cities—sophistication.

Callander has profited from "Dr Finlay." We are glad to know that "Dr Finlay" has enjoyed being in Callander.

"WHO MADE YOU?"

Assistant Producer Miss Sheelagh Rees tells us that she and all connected with Monday and Tuesday's "Dr Finlay" filming at the old Public School were most impressed by the behaviour and ability of the local children who took part. The episode in which the school and Callander children are concerned is called "Who Made You?" and, being the second episode in the new series, should be screened on TV about the end of November of this year. The plot, in this episode, is of the kind that requires no telling beforehand if it is to be enjoyed at the time but it concerns a less fortunate boy who, unable to go to school in the normal manner, is so fascinated by other children and the school "idea" that he is drawn irresistibly to the school playground. One day, he disappears and, in the "Casebook" manner, Dr Finlay rises to the occasion.

Having been given this information by Miss Rees, this might be as good an occasion as any on which to say and mean, yet again, that Callander acknowledges its debt to the BBC, not only for invaluable free publicity, but also for the relief from tedium that so many colourful film folk bring to the place.

Producer of the new series is Douglas Allen, the Director, Ian MacNaughton, and Chief Cameraman James Court.

Quite a number of tourists were thrilled to be able to look on at the shooting of actual scenes and, on Tuesday, saw "Dr Finlay" himself in action before the cameras.

with my fellow child actors in 1966

my earnings from *dr finlay's casebook*

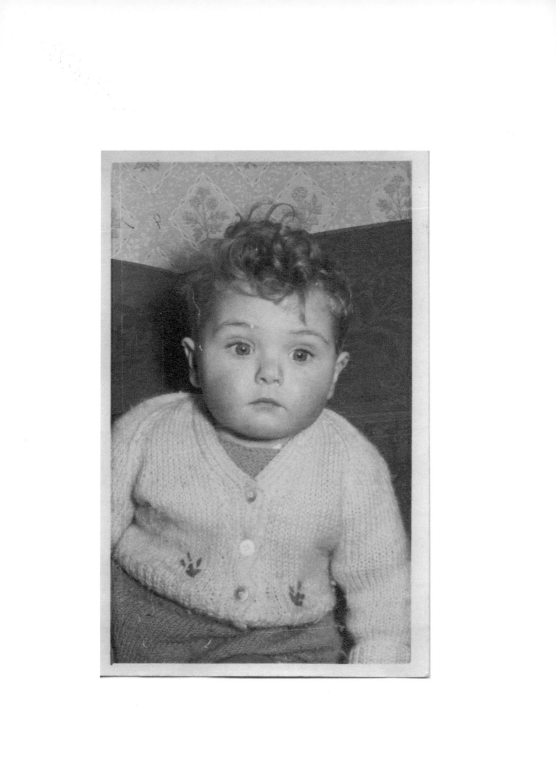

me aged one

ancaster cottage, callander

ancaster cottage, coll

in my own home

a quiet moment at coll pier office

julie and lotti ferry

chilling at a friend's house

rock drummer julie, 1973

still drumming regularly these days
photo credit: ian fergus

on stage, old village hall, arinagour - with west coast rock band *the rise*
photo credit: ian fergus

visiting royal horse guards parade, london

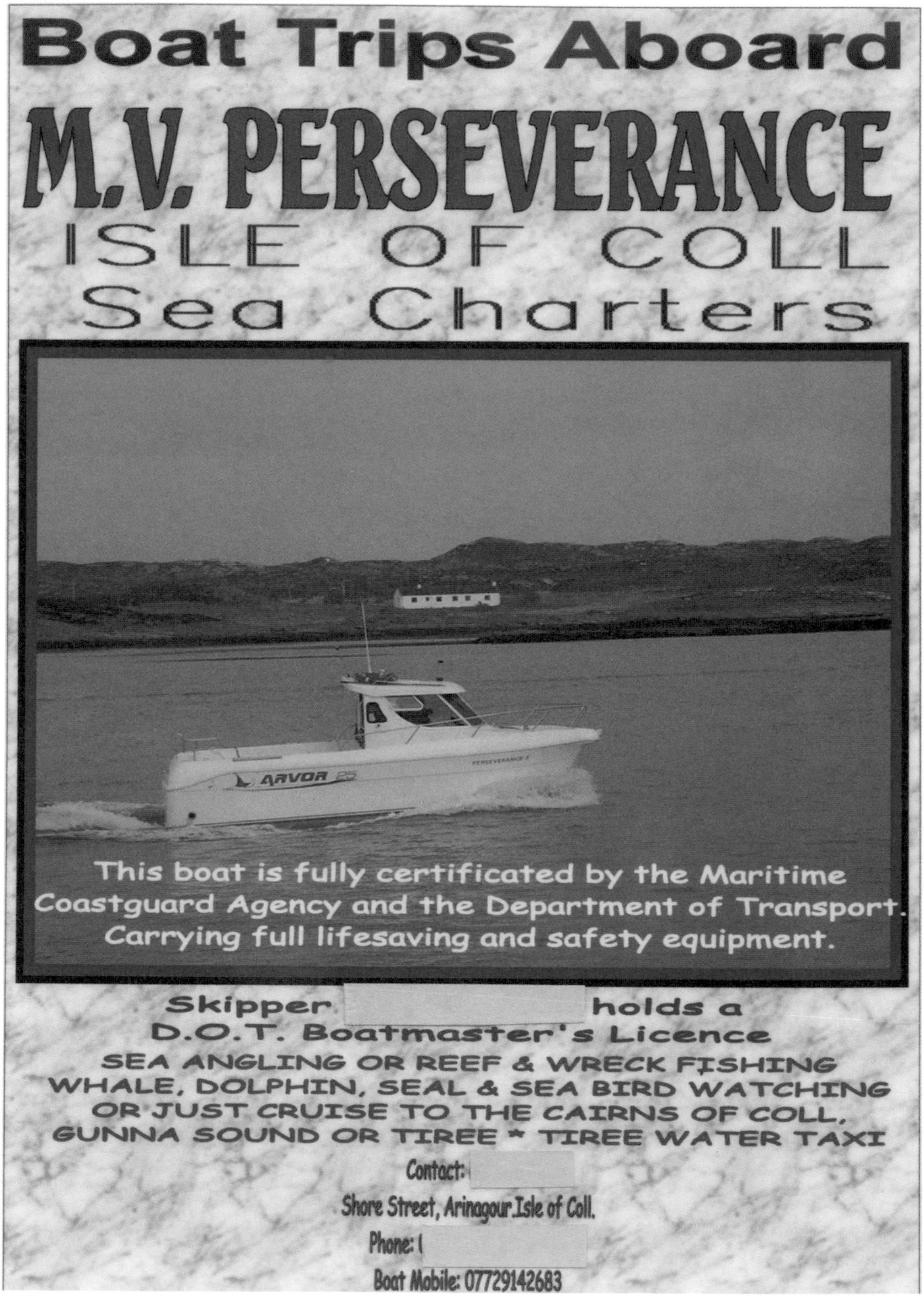

flyer from my time as a skipper

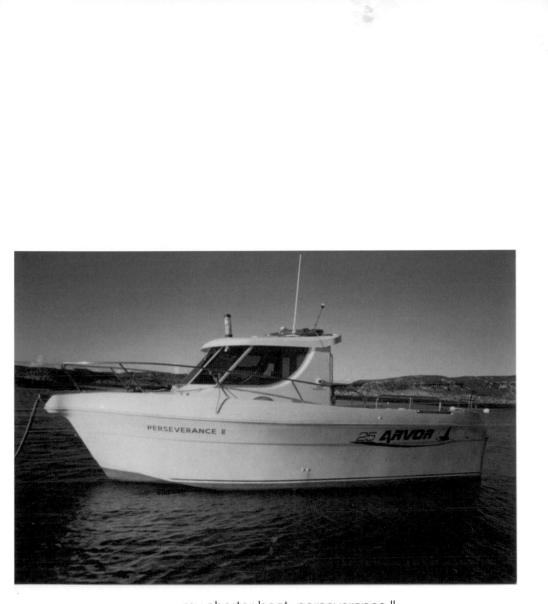

my charter boat, perseverance II

my dear friend marcia

on duty at coll ferry terminal (taken from a ferry)
photo credit: ian fergus

huge fin whale washed up on coll, 2004

To me the entire work situation was unfair. I hadn't asked to be the way I was, and everything I was doing in so-called 'normal life', I felt I was doing well and making a valuable contribution to society. Someone once said to me in the pub, 'I don't care if you are a transvestite or whatever you are. If my house is on fire it makes no difference to me or my family what you are, we will be more than happy for you to come to our rescue.' I thought that was very courageous of him, but it almost sparked a riot as a crowd at the other end of the bar started slagging him off and calling him, among other things, a tranny lover. They then turned their attention to me, saying that if it was their house on fire they wouldn't call me out if they could help it, Truth is, if they called the fire brigade out they would have no control over who turned up in the engine to help them. Luckily no such situation ever arose, but in reality, people are always happy to see you when they really need you, no matter what issues they have with you at other times.

Annoyingly, the guy who had supported me in the pub that night would end up turning against me too, as he was forced to backtrack after threats from the crowd. So now I was aware of someone who wanted to support me, but who was forced to pretend that he too was reluctant to accept me as I was, bowing to pressure from a group who definitely were never going to accept what I was doing. That is a scenario that has followed me throughout most of my journey to becoming Julie.

I fully accept that it will be a long time, if ever, before society as a whole learns to live with and accept those of us who don't conform to what is perceived to be a normal and acceptable lifestyle. But the tough thing for me, and others like me, is that the way we are most definitely isn't a matter of choice. I wasn't dressing up and behaving like a female for a bit of fun. This was who and what I was. I was born that way, and back then, with every year that passed, my female side became ever more powerful even although I still made a few last-ditch attempts to run away from the dilemma.

Some of those futile attempts would cause me to make some of my biggest, most expensive and just plain wrong decisions yet. But what I do know for sure is that I was slowly but surely discarding all male traits, and very gradually developing my female persona. So, regardless of all the trauma, I firmly believe that all the dark and difficult episodes in my life that took place over many years were part of that complicated process which would continue for many more years to come.

It would be another twelve years before this complex process would finally come to a conclusion and then I would have to make a whole new set of tough decisions.

However, going back to the end of my career as a firefighter; it had been about two years since the fateful night when I was stopped by the police and my lifelong secret was blown completely out of the water. In that time I had fended off all attempts by those in the fire service who had wanted rid of me. These included not only the hardliners at the station, but also some of the officers at headquarters, who said that I had brought the service into disrepute. In truth, I actually hadn't done anything wrong. It certainly wasn't a crime to feel that you had been born into the wrong body and then act accordingly by wearing the clothes of the gender that felt right.

I was totally dedicated to a job that I loved and had been trained to do over many years, and in which I had gained a wealth of experience. I was accepted and trusted by the majority of the public to carry out my duties as a firefighter. Even during the two years since I had been unmasked, for want of a better word, there had been good times when I thought I was getting somewhere and educating the lads on the subject. Regardless of any progress I made I would always find myself back at square one, as some people would just find yet more reasons to pick holes in my life. But I persevered and always tried to talk people round again. It is that perseverance that has got me where I am today. Without it, I think I would have crumbled and descended into despair.

Despite my perseverance, I really felt that my time in the fire service was coming to an end; my determination to stay was waning. The sheer pressure and stress on me and the rest of the crew had clearly taken its toll and was wearing us all down. But it sometimes takes an unexpected event to decide an outcome and force your hand, and that was certainly the case with myself and the fire service.

I was out on one of my Julie trips to the city one evening when I mistakenly drove the wrong way down a one-way street and was spotted by a police patrol. I was promptly stopped and charged with driving without due care and attention or something like that. Unfortunately, the media caught wind of this (I'm not sure how, certainly not from me), and my silly mistake was sensationalized in a newspaper a few days later. If I hadn't been dressed as Julie I'm sure no one would have been the slightest bit interested. This gave all the sceptics, including the hardliners in the fire station, exactly what they wanted and they seized the opportunity to make things even more difficult for me.

After a series of difficult and stressful discussions I felt the time had come to accept that my position had become untenable.

Not because the lads were right and I shouldn't be there, simply because of who I was. I had resisted the pressure on me to go for so long because I knew I could do my job and do it well, and I also knew I was morally right. However, something had now changed, and that was the fact that I had been lying to them about being a reformed character. It was all bullshit and deception and I could no longer live with that. I had to make a choice – it was either the fire service or Julie. Up until that moment I had been unable to part with either, but my hand had now been forced and I had to make a decision. There was no contest. I had to follow my heart and continue down the path that had surely been mapped out for me from birth.

With a heavy heart I wrote my letter of resignation to the fire chief at headquarters and he accepted. Astonishingly, I didn't get a single word of thanks, nor any support or acknowledgement of my eleven years of dedicated service. It's hard to imagine this sort of thing occurring today, and to say I was disappointed would be the understatement of the century. I was also sorry when my immediate superior officer at my home station expressed disappointment that I hadn't told him what had happened and that he only found out from the media, but I just hadn't been able to find the courage or the words to speak to him about it at the time. Thankfully, we left it that way and parted on the very best of terms.

Taking the decision to bow out of the fire service was definitely one of the saddest moments of my life. I had been forced to leave the job that I loved passionately; an exciting, demanding, worthwhile, highly skilled and above all, totally rewarding job. As a firefighter people looked up to you; they praised you, they thanked you, and most importantly, they were very grateful that you were there. They could sleep easy in their beds at night in the knowledge that a dedicated crew of brave people would come to their rescue, whatever the problem was, and in any circumstances, at any time of the day or night.

I truly loved being in the fire service – it was a career that I had followed my father into for all the right reasons. I had dreamed of the fire service from a very young age, even through all my struggles with gender issues. Despite believing I was female I had always wanted to be in the fire service, and it turned out to be one of the best experiences of my life and left me a wonderful legacy that would help me through many more tough times ahead. When I was forced to turn my back on it, all I was left with was sadness. I felt I had lost part of me and I could not understand why I had to leave when I had only cared about others. I felt so sorry for myself and for the fact that I had to go just because of a biological quirk – I was a person that society, even in 1992, wasn't ready to accept. All I could do was cry – I would sob myself to sleep every night and sometimes wake in the morning, still crying. I just felt profoundly sorry for myself and struggled to find an answer as to why the world had been so cruel to me. There didn't seem to be one.

My years in the fire service left me with a wonderful, practical and realistic take on life, and gave me an experience that will stay with me for as long as I live. The following words of Sir Eyre Massy-Shaw, who commanded the London Fire Brigade from 1861 to 1892, still ring true today:

A fireman, to be successful, must enter buildings. He must get in below, above, on every side; from opposite houses, over back walls, over side walls, through panels of doors, through windows, through skylights, through holes cut by himself in gates, walls, and in the roof. He must know how to reach the attic from the basement by ladders placed on half-burned stairs, and the basement from the attic by rope made fast on a chimney. His whole success depends on his getting in and remaining there, and he must always carry his appliances with him, as without them he is of no use.

Even in our high-tech world, it is still people who must make the final decisions in any situation. As a firefighter you must use your knowledge and experience to get what you want, resolve a problem, or react to a scenario. And although I had already developed a strong work ethic and great set of principles at a young age, all of this was bolstered by the life skills I learnt in the fire service. Be meticulous, back up your ideas with a plan B, think ahead, expect the unexpected and deal with it promptly, calmly and with decisive actions – and at the end of the task be able to stand back and work out a way of improving on it, in the event that a similar situation should occur in the future. You always have to be prepared to tackle any problem head on and deal with it. These standards have played a big part in shaping the woman I have become today.

chapter seven

moving across the sea

In 1993 our annual holiday to the Isle of Coll was coming round again and Anne and I were becoming increasingly convinced that this was the place that was going to provide me with an escape from my troubles. When we had last visited the island in 1992 we had been told of a building plot for sale and to our surprise it was still available. We decided we would make an offer for it and our offer was accepted. By early 1994 we were the proud owners of a small part of the Hebridean island we both loved, albeit for very different reasons.

For me Coll would always hold happy childhood memories and later in life, during some of my most troubled times, I had found solace and some contentment while I was on the island. Anne's love affair with the Isle of Coll had begun much more recently than mine, when I first brought her there in 1985. She fell in love with the island very quickly, won over by its charm. its beautiful landscape, its stunning beaches, its wildlife, and above all, its people – a mix of indigenous folk and incomers. For the latter, including Anne and I, the pure charm and uniqueness of the place made it somewhere you could escape to, leave the rat race behind and start a new life. This is exactly what we hoped to do at the time, although my reasons for wanting to do so were probably very different to those of other people.

After buying the land we had to find a builder who was willing to construct a house on the island and we also had to find the finance. Anne and I had done pretty well financially over the years. We had worked our way up the property ladder and currently owned a good house. However, building on a remote island wasn't going to be easy and would certainly be expensive. All the materials had to be brought in by ferry and the builders, who would all come from the mainland, had to be put up in accommodation for the three or four months it would take to build the house.

In the meantime I had got a new job with the Water Board at Loch Katrine, about nine miles from Callander. The best thing about the job was that a house came with it, so we were able to sell our house in Callander and sit on the money while we decided how to go about building the house on the island. Our new situation thus gave us breathing space to decide how we were going to proceed with our planned new life on the Isle of Coll. Meanwhile, we had to knuckle down and work to help finance our dream.

Loch Katrine is the main reservoir supplying water to the City of Glasgow, but many of us who worked for the Water Board there were involved in tourism since one of the Water Board's main attractions is the Loch Katrine pleasure steamer, the SS Sir Walter Scott. I crewed on the ship as well as working on the pier and viewed it as good experience if I wanted to fulfil my lifelong desire to work at the much bigger ferry terminal on the Isle of Coll, if and when we went to live there.

Whilst working at the Water Board was a good little job, it was always just going to be a stopgap until we got to the island. We had no idea how long it would take us to finance the house there and build it, it could have been six months or two or three years, we just didn't know, so we both got on with working as hard as we could to get to where we wanted to be. However, my lifestyle was now common knowledge, and my experience in the fire service had taught me to expect more of the same from those I was now working with.

Fortunately for me, my cousin Ian worked for the Water Board too – he was a Grade 1 foreman and was well respected by most of the workforce – and I think it was his presence that protected me to a certain degree, or at least meant that nothing was ever really voiced about my lifestyle, for the most part. Even Ian never broached the subject. This had happened many times before; people just did not want to go there because they didn't know what to say. There were the occasional exceptions and these usually took the form of someone tentatively saying to me, 'Look, we don't mind how you run your life, it's none of our business.' and they would pry no further.

Unfortunately, something happened that directly contradicted that tolerance. I had a work-related disagreement with a colleague and at the end of the somewhat heated discussion, he said to me, 'You shouldn't even be employed here, you're just a fucking pervert, you wcc bastard.' How wrong he was, and how much his abusive words hurt me, but sadly there were no witnesses. It would have been his word against mine, and I knew from past experience that the management wouldn't have believed me anyway. That same person was to get his comeuppance a few months later when, as often seemed to be the case when someone had been blatantly abusive towards me, he turned out to be hiding his own secret and had been using me to deflect suspicion away from himself. Several months after he had a go at me he was convicted of child sex abuse. And he had called me a pervert!

As had happened in the fire service when senior officers accused me of bringing the service into disrepute, instead of trying to understand me, I now found myself facing exactly the same thing at the Water Board. Matters came to a head when they advertised an internal vacancy for a supervisor and I applied. I was shortlisted and duly attended an interview. Almost the very first thing they said to me in the interview was, 'We believe you are into cross-dressing.'

I chose to ignore the fact that this was, of course, inaccurate and asked, 'What's that got to do with me applying for the job?'

The reply was, 'We don't think that the men would want to be told what to do by someone like you.' I then said, 'Why did you even give me an interview in that case?' to which they said they had wanted to clarify the matter.

Needless to say, I didn't get the position. This was 1993 and it's hard to imagine that sort of thing happening today. I felt like the panel of interviewers wanted to humiliate me; all three of them looking across the desk at me and taking notes. This was discrimination at its worst. I knew the situation was absolutely disgraceful, but I didn't kick up about it as I knew no one would back me up, out of fear of reprisal or being ridiculed for helping someone people viewed as a queer.

Anne and I had finally managed to find someone to build our house on the island – someone who had a family link to the island and had built a couple of houses there in the past, so he knew the ins and outs of building there. Over the summer of 1994 we finalized all the details and decided to commence building in the early spring of 1995. Amazingly, the house took only fifteen weeks to complete, helped by dry, sunny weather and increasingly long hours of daylight.

It was during this period that Prince Charles visited the Isle of Coll. He toured the island's only village on foot and his party had to pass our half-built house on their way to visit the local primary school. Sometime before they were due to pass by, the royal protection team appeared on the building site and politely requested that the workmen stop work before the royal party arrived. Inevitably, on the site there was a lot of hammering to be heard, as well as loud music from the radio – they said it might distract the party of royals and dignitaries. As the royal entourage approached, they stopped outside our new house and Prince Charles was heard to say, 'It's good to see new development on the island.' So the house had some sort of royal seal of approval – or at least that's what we liked to think!

Our move to the Isle of Coll was never going to be straightforward. It was difficult financially because Anne and I couldn't just up sticks and move. We still needed money coming in to pay the new mortgage, so we both had to keep working at our jobs on the mainland until we found a way to pay the mortgage and other expenses when we were on Coll. Divine intervention stepped in when Anne was made redundant from the Church of Scotland after the care home she had worked in for more than fifteen years closed down. Luckily she got quite a good redundancy package and this allowed her to move to Coll a few months later and start doing bed & breakfast in the new house, which we had decided to do to help pay the rather large mortgage. For the time being I had to stay at the Water Board to keep the money coming in, but our temporary separation turned out to be quite handy for me. I could now live my life the way I wanted without having to conceal my activities from Anne. It also gave me time to think about the future and showed me how easy I found it to live as a woman when I wasn't upsetting Anne and having to lie all the time.

But we were now heavily committed to the Isle of Coll, and this was supposedly going to be the place that would sort me out and free me from my gender confusion. We were still a good team together, at least most of the time. We were both very enterprising and determined, and had to continue that way now that we had made the brave decision to move off the mainland. I had to try and focus on our future on the Isle of Coll. This would be my final chance to straighten out my life and my dual-gender crisis. If it didn't work, my female side, Julie, would win and I wasn't at the stage yet where I was absolutely certain that was what I wanted. I had to give Coll a chance, and over the next nine years I would make a series of futile attempts to bid Julie goodbye.

When 2004 eventually came, everything would change yet again and my life would become even more complicated, if that were possible. But back in 1995 it was becoming increasingly obvious that I had to join Anne on the Isle of Coll as soon as possible if our plan was ever going to have a chance of working.

One of the most stressful things anyone can do is move house. It's difficult enough moving to somewhere close by, but we had opted to move rather further than that. We needed such a huge change and since our move to Coll was a bid to enable me to get away from my troubles, we decided to call the new house 'Taigh-Solas'. Taigh is Gaelic for house, and Solas echoes solace, which seemed appropriate at the time. It's sad to say, as the years went by, that life in that house became anything but happy or contented.

Although I was still working on the mainland I was able to get to Coll every two or three weeks for a long weekend, and I was always on the lookout for work there, something that would give me enough income to enable me to relocate completely. Since my childhood I had dreamed of working on the pier there, tying the ferry up, so I decided to express an interest to the pier master. The very first time I went to the island with my family in 1965 I had fallen in love with the ship that took us there, and as the years went by, during our summer holidays I was always interested in watching the boats coming into harbour – this was part of the charm of the island. Coming from a land-locked town in central Scotland it was something of a novelty to us. I remember thinking back then that if I ever lived on Coll I would want to work at the pier, as it was called then – it's known nowadays as the ferry terminal.

It was on one of my island weekends that the pier master came round to the house and said that he needed someone to stand in on the pier, as his regular pier hand was off sick. He asked me if I would do it. I almost bit his hand off, so eager was I for the job!

The very next day I was given a quick training course and then I was ready for action. I went straight from tying up and docking the 350-tonne Loch Katrine steamer to tying up a 4,000-tonne Caledonian MacBrayne (CalMac) ferry. I was living my childhood dream! Soon I was being offered more and more stints working on the CalMac pier and this enabled me to give up my job on the mainland and make the move to the Isle of Coll to join Anne. From late 1995 I became a regular worker on the pier and I am still a full-time employee there to this day.

Getting the job on the pier even before I had moved permanently to the island really did seem like a good omen, reinforcing our belief that we were doing the right thing and that our calculated gamble might just have a chance of paying off. But we knew it would only do so if we continued to work hard and take sensible entrepreneurial risks, which is exactly what we did over the next six or seven years, with quite a high degree of success in our various business enterprises – one of which would see us invest over £50,000.   For the next seven years we were highly successful in business, and importantly, for the first two years after I moved to the island I seemed to have conquered my lifelong double-gender problems. Yes, it had been two years since I had felt the urge to go back to being Julie.

I could not have predicted that in 1997 the world we had constructed for ourselves on the Isle of Coll would come crashing down when, literally overnight, a switch was thrown in my brain and I simply woke up one morning and said to myself, 'What the hell am I doing? I am a woman, so why am I doing all this?' I'd known full well what my mind had been screaming at me for years, why was I continuing to make this futile effort to escape from it?

Julie was back, big time and I was more mixed up than ever. The battles I'd had between my male and female sides in the past now paled into insignificance compared with what I now felt. I would do almost anything to be Julie, although, bizarrely, I was still going to extraordinary lengths battling to run away from this urge. I was being torn in two, mostly for the sake of my relationship with Anne, and our business commitments. No matter how strong the pull to be female was, I would be stuck in a never-ending cycle of desperately wanting to be Julie for another few years yet, at the same time half-heartedly trying to avoid temptation. Looking back, I can see that this whole period was a complicated process that I just didn't have any control over. I think I always knew that Julie would eventually win, but at the time I didn't know how or when. Anne and I were about to increase our financial commitment to the island by more than £50,000, and although I didn't know it at the time, this would represent my final attempt to escape Julie's clutches.

In another strange twist to my life I was about to become a sea captain – or to be more precise, a charter boat skipper. Even as I made plans for this, I was also now totally resigned to the fact that in my own mind I was female. The pressure I felt to do what was expected of me was colossal, and the next six years would turn out to be one big facade. I would waste precious time and a lot of money on one of my biggest business ventures yet; all for yet one more vain effort to prove to others that I was something or someone I never had been, and never would be.

As I have said previously, the idea that the Isle of Coll was the answer to my problems had originated almost forty years before when, even as a child, I had found that the island always offered me an escape from all my troubles. The reality was of course, that the same old problems were still there, and it wasn't long before I was exploring new ways to have my cake and eat it. Although I wanted to live the island dream, I also desperately wanted to be Julie. And another thing I had now to think about was whether the people of the Isle of Coll knew about my past. Had word reached Coll from Callander? I didn't detect any signs that it had although I knew it was only a matter of time before word filtered through to the islanders.

Throughout my life women had always been most sympathetic towards me once they knew my secret, and this would continue to be the case. Men who were understanding at first, more often than not would suddenly do a u-turn, usually because of what other men were saying to them; they then became afraid of being ridiculed or even accused of being 'different' themselves. This was something I had dealt with many times over the years, and it usually left me in the most awkward position where I had to accept being suddenly ignored by someone who had previously been friendly towards me. If I had not done so I would have ended up being totally isolated. Thankfully, as the years went on and more and more people got to know about me, I was able to figure out which people would keep me at arm's length without actually commenting. As I had always done, I just got on with life and mostly overcame this silent prejudice. I had to or I would have become even lonelier and alienated myself even more than I already was.

Loneliness would be something that would visit me frequently in the years to come, and I still have to deal with it to this day. But there have always been some people who have been there for me, whether openly or not. By the late 90s there were usually always one or two people willing to give me a chance and accept me as I was. By then people were slowly becoming a wee bit more broadminded. But even now, as I write this in 2014, there's still a very long way to go on that score.

In most ways, living and working on the Isle of Coll really was good for Anne and me. It was hard work, but we were good at that and since we were doing so well financially, we decided to embark on our biggest business venture yet. It became obvious to us that there was a need for someone to take tourists and locals out on boat trips – after all, there was plenty going on in the sea around the island. Apart from fishing, whales, dolphins, seals, sharks and numerous sea birds can all be spotted with a bit of luck, as well as enjoying the beautiful coastal landscapes. We saw a real business opportunity and decided that I would train as a charter boat skipper. Once I had qualified, we bought the first of two fairly substantial boats, and called it Perseverance. To me, this name typified what I was all about, and to this day it is my watchword. The boat soon became well known to locals and tourists alike.

I was reasonably experienced in boat handling, having for some years owned and operated a smaller boat that Anne and I had used for our own pleasure. We had brought the boat with us to Coll, but I hadn't needed any qualifications to operate it as it was only for private use. Running a boat that carried paying passengers was very different. Everything had to have certificates – including me. I went to study at the Firth of Lorne Sea School, run by an ex-deep-sea mariner, Captain Bill Sturrock, who ran a military-like operation. It took me about six weeks to qualify as a skipper, with five weeks of theory and the last week practical boat handling.

I learned about such things as navigation, radio operation, firefighting at sea, first aid at sea, interpreting weather and sea conditions, passenger management in an emergency, maritime law, recognition of navigational aids such as different types of lighthouses, the international buoyage system, and much more. The boat had to comply with the Department of Transport, the Maritime and Coastguard Agency and the Code of Practice for Small Commercial Vessels at Sea, all of which demanded a very high standard from the vessel and its equipment. This was quite an undertaking, and our boat was the first properly licensed charter boat for the Isle of Coll. Thankfully it became an instant success with both locals and tourists alike, not only for pleasure cruises but also as a commuter boat or water taxi between neighbouring islands and even the mainland. More importantly for us at the time, it was a commercial success which was a big relief. The whole venture had cost us in excess of £50,000 – and this was on top of what building the house had cost us.

We were deeply committed to the island and were both well up for making a go of things when suddenly, out of the blue as usual, one day I said to myself yet again, 'What the hell am I doing?'

Even after putting over £200,000 into making a success of our lives on the Isle of Coll, it was becoming increasingly apparent to me with every passing day that my lifelong gender issues weren't going to go away. The degree to which we had committed ourselves to being on Coll meant bugger all to me, but for now I had to go along with it, in the hope that fate would intervene and decide once and for all. For, as I well knew, personal circumstances and unforeseen events could change everything, literally overnight.

For now we were heavily involved in our various business ventures. As well as the boat charter we were also doing bed and breakfast and had a bike hire and taxi/tour business, and that was in addition to me working at the ferry terminal. Looking back on it now, I don't know how we managed it all. We were making a packet though – money was absolutely rolling in and it seemed like we just couldn't fail. Everything we touched turned to gold. Our success hadn't come easily though –we had worked hard all our lives and had taken considerable risks, especially since coming to the island. As well as our financial success, we had also made lots of new friends on Coll and reacquainted ourselves with old ones.

We seemed to be on top of the world, and Coll was the centre of our universe, so what could possibly go wrong?

Well, if the truth be known, there was already a lot that was wrong. Anne and I weren't having big bust-ups or anything like that, but my occasional visits to the mainland when time permitted were now for one reason only – to transform myself back into Julie – something I couldn't risk doing on the island. Everybody knows what you're up to on the Isle of Coll – it's a bit like living in a goldfish bowl. I suppose all small villages are like that, and up until then it hadn't mattered. But now it did.

My gradual return to my female ways was beginning to make Anne uneasy. She could recognize the telltale signs that I was up to my old tricks. And I'm sure that even back then she knew we could not go on like this for ever. But we had invested so much in being on the Isle of Coll that neither of us wanted to face facts at this stage, and we continued to grow our business interests on the island. My boat business was doing so well that I had to get a bigger boat to enable me to carry more passengers. We continued to plough everything into what we were doing, although deep down we both knew exactly where we were headed without actually discussing it.

The next five years would see my male side eliminated once and for all, and Anne would decide quite rightly that she'd had enough and just couldn't take any more.

On one of my increasingly frequent trips to the mainland, I came across a woman who was to help me, encourage me, and offer me a space to be Julie. Helen was one of Anne's best friends and had known for some years about my gender issues. She seemed to understand me and she made me feel comfortable because she totally accepted me as Julie. She allowed me to use her house as a base to go on my city trips, something I hadn't been able to do since moving to the Isle of Coll. We would also have girly nights in with a bottle of wine, watching a movie on TV. So at the time it really did seem like I could have the best of both worlds. That said, when I was with Helen there was always a nagging feeling that I had to get back to Coll, and when I got back there everyone just assumed that I had been away on business or something like that.

Anne, out of loyalty – although that was beginning to wane – kept up that story too, as the alternative would probably have finished us, along with everything we had worked so hard for. We weren't quite at that point yet, though things between us were inevitably becoming more strained and uneasy.

Although I had intuitively known from a very young age that I should have been a woman, it is quite astonishing to me now that even by that stage of my life on the Isle of Coll, I didn't actually know very much about my 'condition', or any of the terms used to describe someone like me. This lack of knowledge was caused by a combination of circumstances. Society largely disapproved of people like me, I was also in denial about who and what I was and there was also very little information freely available about transgender issues in general. All I knew was that I had had a very complicated and traumatic life.

I was in my twenties before I heard the words 'transvestite' (which I was not) and 'transsexual', which I was coming to realize I might be. This turned out to be almost the case, but not quite. I had never really mixed with others like me and the few times that

I did, I just didn't see myself as having anything in common with them. So even after nearly forty years I still didn't know how I was going to change or progress things – that is, how I was ever going to become my true female self.

This all changed when I was at Helen's one evening and we were sitting having a bottle of wine and a good girly blether, and she said to me out of the blue, 'Well, when are you going to get a sex change, then?'

Even after everything I had been through over nearly forty years, I just couldn't comprehend that question. I had always known that some day I would be the woman that I always should have been, but until the moment Helen asked me, I honestly had never thought about the nitty-gritty of how I would achieve this. From that day on I began to think about my life in a completely different way. I had arrived somewhere new, somewhere I needed to be, thanks to Helen. It was one thing going through all of those years unconsciously eliminating all things male in favour of more and more things female, but it was another thing entirely arriving at a place in my mind where I knew how to make the ultimate transformation actually happen.

However, Anne and I still had all of our joint business commitments and we were still married, and at this point I had no idea how I was going to get out of the predicament I was in, and finally break free to do what my mind had been telling me I needed to do for so long. But within a couple of years Anne would bring about a dramatic change in our lives that would free us both from what had become a troubled relationship. Having started off, to all intents and purposes, as a normal man and woman falling in love for all the right and usual reasons, Anne and I now found ourselves in an unbearable situation. The fact that our relationship had descended into a complicated and unhappy marriage is something I take full responsibility for, and I am still to this day deeply sorry for what I put Anne through. But I was what I was, I was born that way, and I had absolutely no control over it.

Since we were now living on the island where we had taken our holidays for so long, we suddenly found there was nowhere obvious to go away to on holiday, and even if we did, we could not go away for too long, due to our commitments. Because of this we found ourselves visiting Anne's auntie in Preston for a break now and then. This was quite handy for me as I was close to Blackpool, the place I had spent some time many years ago as Julie, and also as a drummer in several bands there. So this was a great opportunity to go back to my old stomping ground.

In the same way I had wondered if word about me had spread to Coll from Callander, I also wondered if the revelations about me had spread to Anne's relations in Preston. I thought this unlikely, so I used to take an extra suitcase with me full of my female gear. Astonishingly, I kind of got away with this because Anne wanted to spend lots of time with her aunt, giving me the chance to do my own thing on the nights I wasn't with them. I would tell Anne's aunt Ella that I was going to Blackpool to listen to live music, which was technically true, but what I didn't tell her was that I would be going out as a woman. I would make myself up in our bedroom in Ella's house and disappear out of the front door when I was ready.

Meanwhile, Anne would feel obliged to cover for me although she was generally not at all happy about it. I was really pushing my luck and there was a point where she threatened to tell Aunt Ella.

To be honest, in a way I would have been glad if she had done. But it never came to that, though I'm sure Ella had an inkling; when I came home in the early hours of the morning she was always waiting up for me. I'm sure she could see the remnants of makeup on my face; she would look at me strangely, almost implying she knew something was going on and would then interrogate me as to what I had got up to on my night out. This sort of scenario was something that I had played out hundreds of times over the years; I had learned many years ago how to deflect scrutiny and would rapidly move on to another subject to divert prying questions and lines of inquiry.

I did have an increasing desire just to tell all, as it would have been a weight off my shoulders. However, the fear of negative consequences held me back – at least for the time being. I just didn't want Anne's relatives to know at that time.

On one of our journeys home from Preston Anne and I had our first-ever meaningful conversation about our situation. I had, as ever, been pushing my luck and leaving Anne with her aunt while I did my own thing, and it was becoming apparent to me that Anne was probably not going to allow this to happen again. I didn't want to go back to the Isle of Coll, because I just didn't want to go back to being that little bloke who did the boat trips any more. As far as I can remember, this trip was the first time that we discussed the possibility that I might some day have a sex change, and although we had at that point been together for more than twenty years it was an extraordinarily difficult and awkward conversation.

On that trip Anne also accused me of using her as a front for all those years; a cover for what I was really doing. She was right in a way although I hadn't planned it like that. Despite feeling very uncomfortable, by the time we got home I felt we had achieved more in that seven hours, in terms of squaring our situation with each other, than we had in the previous twenty years together. I think we both knew from then on that things would change. We didn't yet quite know how, but we both knew our lives were going to be vastly different from that moment on.

As events transpired, in early 2002 Anne moved back to Callander on a semi-permanent basis, leaving me to struggle on with our commitments. This was not sustainable and we soon decided to begin winding up our various enterprises. The first to go were the bike hire and the taxi/tours, followed by the bed and breakfast business, but I kept the boat charter going and I was still working at the ferry terminal. Shortly after that, we agreed to sell the house we had built on the island. This decision came with a lot of tears from us both. Building that house had been a dream come true for us both at the time. When the house was sold, I suppose that marked our official separation. Anne split her time between the Isle of Coll and Callander, staying with friends, and I rented a small cottage in Arinagour, the only village on the island. I was left not only with the boat charter business, but also, and more importantly, with our beloved cat, Geal – the Gaelic word for white; unsurprisingly, she was so named because she was pure white.

At that time Geal was the only companion I had in the whole world and she meant everything to me. I treasured her until the day she died at the age of seventeen, which completely broke my heart. If I was to return in another life then I would come back as a female cat because cats fit the bill for me exactly. They are determined, tenacious, enterprising, opportunistic, meticulous, and above all, fiercely independent. Yes, that's me – so please may I come back as a cat?

Although our split had been traumatic, Anne's leaving opened up a whole new world to me, and freed Anne from what had become an unbearable situation; she was also thinking of me too, because that's the selfless type of person she is.

The very next year I took the first subtle step towards changing direction. I gave up my boat business and duly sold the boat a few months later. This gave me substantial financial security at a time when I had no idea as to how I was going to proceed. I knew that some day I would become a woman, but unbelievably, I still didn't know how I was going to achieve this.

I hadn't yet approached a professional in the field of sex-changes and at the time I wasn't computer literate so I couldn't research anything on the Internet. Instead, I fell in to a lonely limbo of having the freedom at last to get on with changing my life, but having no clue about how to move forward. This got me thinking that perhaps I should have mixed with other transsexuals when I had had the chance, on my visits to the city over the years. I now lived on a remote island and my work there didn't allow me to go to the mainland very often.How was I ever going to achieve what seemed like an impossible dream?

It would be yet another woman who would take me under her wing and help me. Marcia Gratwick was from Northern Ireland and she first came to the island as a passenger on a cruise ship, the Hebridean Princess, which regularly calls at Coll. Marcia soon fell in love with Coll and eventually bought a house there. Amongst all my other business interests on the islands I also did small-scale building maintenance, and she asked me to do some work on her newly-acquired house. I had initially met her in the pub and we hit it off right away. Even after I finished the work at her house

I continued to visit her and we became close friends. I felt so comfortable with her that I decided one day to tell her everything. Luckily, she was totally supportive, and like Helen in Callander, I had many girly nights in with Marcia, and she became one of my most loyal friends on the island. The downside was that our girly nights in had to be a secret because I still wasn't out in the open on the island. I do think some people were beginning to put two and two together, and I know I was being talked about, Marcia had told me this was the case. As usual, no one dared say anything to me on the subject – partly because they just weren't sure whether it was true, and partly because they were too polite, or saw it as none of their business.

chapter eight

the point of no return

It was now forty years since, at the age of seven, I had first begun to realize that something was wrong with how I felt about my body. The monumental struggle that was to follow has taken its toll on me and there are still times when I look back and really do wonder how I made it through. In the early years I simply didn't know why I felt the way I did or why people treated me differently. Then life became a constant battle with my inner self and still no answers. This was followed by years of trying to suppress my female side and then being overcome by the need to express it, with all the highs and lows that entailed as I struggled to keep up the appearance of 'normality'. I lived like that for years, knowing all the time it was inevitable that some day I would give in and follow what my body and mind had been telling me was natural for me. Although deep down I always knew the day would come, I had no idea how or when that would happen.

Finally, after my forty-year-long traumatic journey, I felt like it might be possible to sort my life out. I had been to hell and back, and then some, and my nearest and dearest family and friends had also been dragged through a quagmire of difficult, complicated and heartbreaking circumstances. They had had to come to terms with a situation they had never dealt with before and which, for the most part, they could never comprehend. Why would a man want to become a woman?

I had to make a decision one way or another, I had cried my self to sleep at nights for forty years and I now desperately had to find a way out. I had finally come to my breaking point. Yes, I had been here before, but something was different this time. I was at the stage where, when I went to sleep at night I thought, if I don't wake up in the morning that will be a release. All my grief and turmoil would be over and I would be free at last. I knew that these suicidal feelings were dangerous, no matter how good the thought of being free felt. The time had come for me to follow my heart and pull myself back from the brink of total meltdown.

The next few months would call on all the experience I had gained over the years, and confirm my utter determination to forge ahead, even with the odds stacked hugely against me. I would encounter fierce opposition to the path I chose – fiercer than anything I had experienced up to that point – and strangely, or perhaps it was naivety on my part, the people I thought I could count on and trust to support me would be the ones who turned against me or who were just not there when I needed them most.

I really felt I had reached the point of no return. With my life as I had known it disappearing before my eyes, I made that quantum leap. The strangest feeling came over me as I made the decision to follow the path I felt had always been mapped out for me. I now felt that something, or someone, was looking after me and making sure I was doing the right thing. The long process I had gone through, experimenting with my male and female sides, had finally ended, leaving me in no doubt as to what my gender really was. I was female and there was no getting away from it. That lifelong struggle of fighting against my femininity was finally over – at a huge cost to me and those close to me.

The first part of my incredible journey was over, and the second part was about to begin. This would turn out to be every bit as harrowing as the last, albeit in a very different way.

I had finally made a decision that would at last set me on the road to making the physical changes to my body necessary to complete this second part of my journey. I knew that I couldn't go back to the way my life had been and that really put me under tremendous pressure: what if I couldn't find anyone to help me? And what if they didn't want to know and told me I needed psychological help of some sort? What if they wanted to try and cure me of something? I'm lucky, I think if any of my fears had been realised that may well have been the end of me.

Every minute of every day was now taken up with thoughts of how I was going to achieve my goal and become a woman. All of a sudden I felt like I had wasted the past forty years, and I wanted everything to change immediately. At the same time I knew nothing would be simple or quick, even although I had no idea of what an uphill task still lay ahead of me.

The one thing I did know was that the only person in the world I could approach was my GP. She was a young and enlightened doctor, and I had been a patient of hers since she had arrived on the island, five years previously, so she knew me well. Memories of the disgraceful treatment dished out to me by ignorant doctors in Callander in the 1980s still lingered, but I was confident that my new GP's attitude would bear no resemblance to the lack of empathy I had experienced back then. Nevertheless, I was extremely nervous about approaching her, but I had to. I knew there was absolutely no alternative if I was going to go ahead with my plan.

It was now autumn and the buzz of a busy summer was over, thus giving me more time to pluck up enough courage and go and see the GP. For two or three weeks I rehearsed what I was going to say to her when I finally bit the bullet and made the appointment; day after day, for hours on end, I was becoming more and more confused. I kept changing my script and then getting all upset because I felt I would never be able to explain myself clearly to her.

One night I went to bed and just lay on my back, wide awake for hours, my whole life seeming to pass in front of me. After many hours I finally fell asleep, still crying. When I woke, quite late the next morning, something seemed to have shifted inside me and after breakfast I drove to a place called the Windy Gap, on the north-west of the island.

From the sand dunes I walked down to Gallanach Beach where I had spent some of my happiest days as a child on holiday in the 1960s, mostly before the years of confusion really started. Inevitably I ended up in floods of tears as those childhood memories came flooding back, but after about half an hour I pulled myself together and walked back to the car and drove straight to the doctor's surgery. I remember I went straight in and directly to the reception desk, at which point the doctor came through as she had heard me come in.

I said, 'Can I talk to you about something?' and she replied, 'Ok, you'd better come through'.

We sat down and she asked, 'What's on your mind?'

My rehearsed script didn't even come into my head. I just explained everything to her as simply as I could. I told her about my whole situation without having a clue as to how she would react. I needn't have worried because she was totally sympathetic, even enthusiastic, and was willing to try and help me from the very first moment I spoke to her about what I wanted to do.

Astonishingly, before the end of that day she had tracked down the only NHS clinic in Scotland – the Sandyford Clinic in Glasgow – that specialized in dealing with people with my kind of gender issues. She spoke to someone there who said they would send out an initial appointment date for me. This would be the first of dozens of appointments at specialist clinics over the next two years.

For the first time in my entire life I felt that now I really had someone willing to help me. Also, for the first time I thought that maybe society actually had made some progress – the NHS was at last treating my gender issue as a medical condition. Unfortunately, I would also discover over the next few years that some elements of society hadn't really changed that much at all.

After a couple of weeks the Sandyford Clinic sent my first appointment date, the 6th of January 2004. I would be seeing a sexual health psychologist who specialized in this field, to ascertain if I really was what I thought or felt I was. Waiting to speak to the psychologist I felt the same fear that I had felt before I met with my GP. I was petrified that he was about to slam shut the door my GP had opened for me. He was the one person who could have challenged my belief in what I thought I was. He asked me questions going right back to my childhood. 'How did you feel way back then? Did you think you should have been a little girl, even then?'

I said I had never liked hanging out with the boys and preferred watching the girls all of the time, and wished I could be like them. He asked about my sex life as an adult, and asked if I was attracted to men or woman. I said I was attracted to men, but that I felt for sure that I wasn't homosexual. I explained that I never felt comfortable when in a sexual situation with a woman because I felt I was the same as her. He asked me about my habits, what did I like to read, what did I like to talk about? He asked about my inner feelings, my thoughts and my dreams. I explained that my whole life had been consumed by my inner turmoil, and in my own mind I couldn't escape the nagging confusion which was ripping me apart. As for my dreams, well, I told him that when I went to sleep each night I longed to waken in the morning and find I was a woman. His questions became more and more direct as the conversation went on.

'How do you feel when you look at your naked body in the mirror?'

I replied, 'I can't look at it, I'm disgusted. I can't accept it somehow.'

'How do you feel when you dress in women's clothes? Are you sexually aroused?'

I said, 'No, not at all. All I know is that dressing as a woman just feels so natural to me.'

After meeting with him for over an hour he concluded that I was indeed transsexual.

I was so happy at the diagnosis I literally skipped back to my car. I went back home to Coll with a great sense of relief and satisfaction.

This was the first time in my life that a sexual health professional had confirmed that I was what I had always known I was. But a final and more accurate diagnosis would be agreed upon at a future appointment with another psychologist, in consultation with my doctor at the Sandyford. That final diagnosis was something I had previously never even heard of – something called 'gender dysphoria'. At last, after forty years of total confusion, I had the answer that had eluded me throughout those unbearably difficult years.

chapter nine

a transsexual by any other name

The following definition of gender dysphoria is taken from a website dedicated to this and similar issues:

What is Gender Dysphoria?

> *Gender Dysphoria is a general term for persons who have confusion or discomfort about their birth gender. Milder forms of gender dysphoria cause incomplete or occasional feelings of being the opposite sex. The most intense form of the condition, with complete gender reversal, is called transsexualism. A transsexual is a male or female who has a lifelong feeling of being trapped in the wrong body. The identification with the opposite sex is so strong and persistent that the transsexual feels the only way to achieve peace of mind is to change the body to match the mind. Some go through the process of living in the chosen role with the help of hormones, eventually leading to sex reassignment*

surgery. Others seek help to learn to live with their
secret feelings with less guilt and shame.

What Causes Gender Dysphoria?

Although life experiences may affect the outward
expression of gender behaviour, there must be some
underlying changes in the brain for transsexualism
to occur. The precise cause of the condition is
unknown. It is now generally accepted that some
changes likely occur before birth, causing parts of
the transsexual's brain to develop in the pattern
opposite to that of his or her physical sex.

Unlike my first experience with the NHS, back in the 80s when
Anne had spoken to our GP about the way I felt, there was now a
considered and professional approach to gender dysphoria. NHS
opinion, at least in some cases, was that by treating the condition
immediately, precious time and money could be saved in the
longer term by avoiding all sorts of future psychological and other
health issues. This did not mean that someone could just walk into
a clinic and say, 'I think I'm transsexual' and be told, 'Ok, you can
have a sex change operation on us.'

It wasn't that simple and I was still worried that some doctor,
somewhere, might conclude that I wasn't someone who had been
born into the wrong body with the wrong genitalia, and tell me to
go away. Thankfully that didn't happen.

However, it was still necessary for the NHS to make sure beyond any doubt whatsoever that I was indeed suffering from gender dysphoria. After all, once it was decided that this was the case, I would undergo an operation that is totally irreversible. Once it's done, it's done and even although the doctors were as sure as I was that I was a woman in a man's body, I still had to prove this to them by living successfully as a woman for two years, in every aspect of my life.

I was subjected to rigorous checks and a succession of psychological tests, each one designed to reiterate what the previous one had found – namely, incontrovertible clinical and psychological evidence that I was female.

Marcia had told me that people in our small island community were speculating about what was going on with me although no one was really sure exactly. I do think that some at least had an inkling about what was happening.

My 48th birthday was coming up on the 16th of February and since I was now living on my own, I wasn't planning anything. There was a knock on the door that evening and it was a bunch of friends I'd known since Anne and I had come to Coll, nine years previously. We had stayed friends after I separated from Anne; they'd come to celebrate my birthday and brought food and drink with them. It was a nice surprise and we had a really good night – we all liked a good drink and a laugh.

The more you have to drink, the braver you get and the more you say, and one of the women, at the time one of my closest friends, rubbed her hand up and down my arm and said, 'I know you shave your arms.'

I said, 'Yes – you know why, don't you?' and she replied, 'Yes.'

I then said, 'I'm probably going to make a big change in my life soon', and her response was, 'It won't make any difference to us.'

That gave me great hope at the time, and I thought, 'Yes, everything is going to be alright.'

Sadly, when I finally made my big change, I received a very rude awakening when some of these friends dropped me like a hot potato, turning their backs on me at a time when I really needed my friends around me. Although the passage of time has made things a bit easier between us, my relationship with the group is nothing like it was before I became a woman.

However, that was all to be faced in the future. In 2004 I took the momentous step of agreeing with the Sandyford Clinic that my official start date for living as a woman would be the 1st of May. Before I felt able to do that, there was one thing that I needed to attend to quickly: I needed a new name. I already had my female Christian name of Julie, given to me by Anne, many years previously, but I now needed a surname. For this, I cast my thoughts back twenty-four years to my early trips to Edinburgh as a female, and to the person who had at that time taken me under her wing. Sadly, she had since died, but she was one of the few people who had instantly believed in me and accepted me for what I was. She was Sue Clarke and taking her surname was an easy choice to make, and one I am very proud of. In March 2004 I signed the final self declaration forms at the General Register Office in Edinburgh, and I was now known legally as Julie Clarke.

Although I still had a mountain of red tape to contend with, another positive outcome was that, along with the name change, I was also now certified legally as being female. This allowed me to change everything from my passport – which now had F for female on it to bank accounts, driving licence, insurance policies and everything else official. This all had to be certified by declarations from the legal and health professionals concerned. I wasn't just changing my name, I was changing everything: my identity, and most importantly, my gender. I was now legally recognized by the authorities as being female, even if I still hadn't changed physically.

Before those final and permanent changes could be made to my body, changes I had longed for nearly all of my life, I still had to prove I could live successfully as a woman within society for two years. For some reason I had it in my head that I would have to leave Coll to do this, and go and live in the city. Glasgow was my top choice because that was where the Sandyford sexual health clinic was and I thought it would be easier just to blend in with the crowd, like I had always done in the past.

My deadline of the 1st of May, when I would officially change and start living as a woman was only about five or six weeks away and it was becoming more and more apparent to me that moving was not going to be very easy. I would have to find somewhere to live in Glasgow and I would need to try and find a job there too. Although I had more than £50,000 in the bank, this was my life savings and I didn't want to just fritter it away. Two people in particular on the island were questioning why I felt I had to leave; this was my home. One was my close friend Marcia, who didn't want to lose her best friend. She told me that she was looking forward to being able to go out to the pub with Julie instead of meeting her behind closed doors. She wanted to go on shopping trips to the mainland with Julie and go on holiday as two female friends together. She also wanted to show me how to really live as a woman – and that's exactly what she did as time went on.

The other person who helped persuade me to stay on the island was my GP, Dr O'Neill, who had enthusiastically supported me from the beginning, when I first approached her in late November 2003.

Just as Marcia had done, she said, 'You shouldn't have to leave. This is your home and what about all your friends?'

I said, 'I'll probably lose most of them.'

To which she said, 'Well if you do lose some, they probably weren't real friends anyway and even if you lose half of them, you'll still have more friends here than you'll ever have in Glasgow, where you'll be totally on your own.'

I realized they were both right and over the next few days I began to calm down and start to plan properly for my next big milestone: the 1st of May when I would be reborn as Julie Clarke.

There were now only four weeks to go and I still had lots to do. I have to say that I was pretty nervous because I didn't really know how people were going to react when they met me for the first time as Julie. The whole community now knew what I was going to do at the end of the month, and some folk had been asking me about it and were saying, 'We don't care what you do, it's got nothing to do with us,' and so forth. I knew from a lifetime of experience that some would see the reality very differently and not find it so easy to deal with. But I was prepared for that, or at least I thought I was, as there was going to be tough times ahead for quite a while after my big change. For now, though, I just had to get on with the business of notifying everyone I was associated with as to my intentions; ploughing through the red tape just went on and on. Very importantly, my employers, Caledonian MacBrayne (CalMac), had pledged their full support. The company admitted that they had never had to deal with anything like this before, but they were willing to embrace my situation wholeheartedly – and still do to this day, even to the point of supporting and protecting me on numerous occasions.

With only about a week to go before I would be living openly as Julie Clarke, I had taken a few days off work to do some last-minute stuff in Oban, the nearest mainland port. It would in fact be my last visit to the mainland as a man; the next time I would go there I would be Julie.

I've been through some strange episodes in my troubled life and what happened when I arrived in Oban was certainly one of those, though it kind of reinforced to me that I was doing the right thing. Anyway, it was lunchtime and I was walking along the seafront in Oban, heading for a restaurant on the north pier. The road was quite busy and for whatever reason I turned round and looked back along the street. There was plenty of traffic, but I didn't notice anyone walking behind me, though as I continued walking I became increasingly aware of loud footsteps behind me. They were getting closer and closer which I found odd because when I had looked back only moments ago there had been no one there. It got to the point where I was sure that someone was right on my heels, so I turned round and was startled to find this little bloke, right behind me.

I have absolutely no idea where he came from, but he came right up to me, looked me in the eye and said, 'Don't ever look back – that's all over now, let it go.' He then turned and disappeared into what now seemed like a crowd of people. It really freaked me out at the time, and is something I've turned over in my mind, time and time again, and which still makes me feel very emotional. I genuinely have no idea who that man was, but I firmly believe it was my old self giving his blessing to the new me. And it remains one of the strangest moments of my journey so far.

There were now just two days to go before I would, for the first time, step out of the front door of my cottage in Arinagour as Miss Julie Clarke. I was very apprehensive to say the least. I had no idea how people were really going to react, but even with this on my mind I was already beginning to feel some sense of relief. The tug of war between my male and female sides was finally over. All the big decisions had now been made, and I no longer cried myself to sleep as I had done most nights for the past forty years. The deep anxiety and heart palpitations that I had been having had also miraculously disappeared.

I was feeling liberated, upbeat and very positive about my future. For the first time in my life I was clear in my mind about where I was going, and a huge weight had been lifted from my shoulders. I also knew I still had an uphill battle ahead of me, but I now felt strong and ready to take on the world that had conspired against me for most of my life. Nothing was going to stop me now.

The first of May finally arrived, and I spent that day discarding clothing and other items associated with my past that I wouldn't be using again, and generally sorting myself out. I was now officially living as Julie Clarke, but it wouldn't be until the following morning that I would emerge from my cottage as the woman I had become. There was a ferry due in on that day, so I would need to report to the ferry terminal as usual, and since everyone knew I would now be living as a woman they were probably expecting me to make my first public appearance dressed accordingly.

There was actually no striking difference to my appearance on that first working day as Julie. The uniforms at the ferry terminal are exactly the same for men and women and I tried to keep my makeup quite low-key, initially when I was at work. The day was actually quite disappointing for me, given the huge psychological build up there had been and I also suspect it may have been a disappointment for those people around me who were expecting to see a dramatic change take place, literally overnight.

Two weeks later I had to go to Dr O'Neill to have my ears syringed and when she was finished we had a chat about how everything was going. I explained that I was finding it difficult at work as I didn't look much different, but she said, 'It doesn't matter how you look at work or what people think, it's how you feel, and that's all that matters.'

She was absolutely right. After that conversation I began to use more makeup, and my hair was also growing longer since I now had no need to hide what I was doing. I began to feel better and better as my optimism and confidence grew daily.

I was also painfully aware that my sex change was having a huge impact on the rest of the island. There were those who were happy for me, there were those who were apathetic, and there were definitely some who were didn't approve of what I was doing. Some people came up to me and said that they thought I was very brave and they respected me for what I was doing. Some were still polite towards me, but that was as far as they went, and there were those who now couldn't look me in the eye. There were also some people who avoided me altogether, but there was only one person on the island who verbally abused me at the time. Now, ten years later, even that person speaks to me openly and easily. For the most part I was doing remarkably well considering the issue I had brought to the community. I was very aware indeed that my situation was always going to be difficult for them, as well as for me. And I completely understand that everyone was entitled to their opinion. At the end of the day everyone had their own way of dealing with it and if I upset or offended anyone I am deeply sorry.

One or two folk dealt with my gender change by bringing a bit of humour into the situation. Being an island, Coll has a couple of quite big commercial fishing boats, and the fishermen are pretty tough and usually have plenty to say about most things that happen on the island. One of them, Innes, is always telling jokes and is quite outspoken, and I have always been quite friendly with him, but he was having a job getting his head round my change to Julie Clarke. Anyway, I was with Marcia on one of my very first pub outings as Julie and when we arrived at the pub, Innes was sitting there drinking with his partner and some other friends. It was the first time he had met me as Julie.

I said, 'Hello Innes', and he just looked at me. I was expecting some sort of joke or a comment at least, but he just sat there silently; he simply didn't know what to say. So I continued, 'Well, Innes, it's the first time I've ever known you stuck for words.' Any awkwardness was quickly avoided when the rest of the group resumed their conversations.

The next day Innes came in to the office at the ferry terminal, as he often does, and we had a hilarious conversation. One of the things he said to me was, 'I don't know what to call you – is it he or she?'

I said, 'You couldn't try she by any chance?'

He replied, 'No, not yet, I'll have to get used to it first, so I'll call you "shim" for now, if that's ok.'

I said, 'Yes, that's fine for now.' I reckoned it was if it helped him get his head round my new life. And that was how Innes dealt with my becoming Julie – he wasn't taking the piss, just using humour to help get him through something that was a difficult situation for him.

The following week he went off to the mainland with his partner on a shopping trip, and when they returned they came into the office and presented me with a small package which they told me they thought I might like. They looked on eagerly while I opened it and I was absolutely thrilled to see that it was a mug emblazoned with the words 'I WOULD RATHER BE A WOMAN!'

Some islanders changed my Christian name slightly, calling me Jules rather than Julie. I think they found this easier because the name sounded like it could be a boy's or a girl's name. This was something that I had no control over, but I thought if it helps people and they find it easier to address me, I'll just have to accept it. This version of my new name also spread to the mainland; people in Oban were starting to call me Jules as well. And to this day I am mostly known as Jules, even by my own family, although a small percentage of folk call me Julie, and I always introduce myself as Julie when I meet someone for the first time. Most people, after a couple of weeks, also start to call me Jules, because that's what they hear everyone else calling me. Jules is fine I suppose, but when I'm at work at the ferry terminal, my ID badge reads 'Julie Clarke'.

There was one person who was definitely there for me and prepared to stand by me through thick and thin, and that was my friend Marcia. One or two of my other friends weren't scared to be seen out with me and also gave me a lot of support, but it was Marcia who was by my side most of the time. She said to me at the time, 'We have to put up a united front and show people that you can live among them normally as a woman.' So we increased our trips out to the pub for meals and drinks just to make a point. I hoped that the more I continued to mix with the people I had known before my change, the easier my new circumstances would become for all concerned. By and large this strategy proved fairly successful.

I remained best friends with Marcia and we even travelled together all over Europe; we both liked city breaks; good hotels, restaurants, wine bars, museums, and lots of shopping – boutiques of course. Our favourite way of getting to Europe was by ferry from Rosyth to Zeebrugge which took seventeen hours overnight. This suited us down to the ground. The ferry was like a small cruise ship with restaurants, bars and live music. We'd go to bed around midnight and when we got up in the morning we'd arrived at our destination, it was great. Our first stop was always Bruges where we would spend a couple of nights and from there we toured Europe in a sort of clockwise direction, visiting major cities like Paris and Barcelona.

Marcia and I made this trip several times and I remember once, on the ferry to Zeebrugge, I had a blast from my past when I spotted two couples I knew from Callander, my home town that I had left nine years previously. At the very same time that I saw them on the lower deck, one of the men in the group happened to look up to the top deck where I was standing with Marcia and clearly saw me too, even although my appearance had changed considerably. Davy, who is a bit older than me, was the person I had bought my first drum kit from when I was just fourteen, so we even had a history of sorts. I had spotted them but I had no way of knowing whether they recognised me.

I didn't see them again until later that evening in the bar when they came over and said hello, and it was clear they had recognised me earlier. We had a few drinks together and chatted a bit. They told me they were amazed at the change in me and said that it was for the better, which was good to hear from people from my hometown. After that we only saw them once, briefly, as we disembarked from the ferry the next morning, but a few weeks later an old friend from Callander phoned me to say that Davy and his friends had spread word all over town that they had met up with me. This was apparently a big deal at the time because they were the first people from Callander to have met me as Julie. Although I had no way of knowing what was actually said, I felt quite pleased that they had gone back to Callander and told everybody what I was now like.

It wasn't only in Callander that I was the subject of much local gossip – I may also have been the most talked-about person in the history of the Isle of Coll. But gradually, as other local issues came along, my story started to be diluted and was no longer the first thing on people's lips. As well as the usual stuff, like people having affairs and other boring trivia, fortunately for me, a great good-time story and a welcome distraction was just around the corner.

The story was actually born out of a natural tragedy, and although when it ended I would again be the focus of attention, that attention turned out to be more positive than negative. It was early in the summer of 2004, and a massive story was breaking on the island. Word reached us that a huge whale had been washed up on a beach on the Atlantic coast at the west end of the island, but it was quickly established that the unfortunate animal had died and its body had been washed even further up the beach, making it easily accessible on foot. An increasing number of folk, myself included, headed down to look at the poor creature, which was identified as a fin whale, the second-largest species of whale on the planet after the blue whale. This one was sixty-five feet long, which is the same length as an articulated lorry, and it weighed about thirty tonnes.

As I was there soon after it beached and before the tide covered it again, I was able to take some great photos of it, but although it was one of the most impressive things I had ever seen, it was also one of the saddest. It was heartbreaking to look into its huge eyes and imagine it roaming the ocean. Sadly, its life had ended on a beach on my island. I went home that night and wept as I remembered seeing my own reflection in its huge staring eye and that's something I'll never forget.

The whale inevitably attracted the attention of the national press who had come initially to report on the beaching of the animal, though the story quickly turned into a Whisky Galore! caper that became almost bigger than the whale story itself. Islanders were sneaking around in the middle of the night stealing body parts from the unfortunate beast – the prized parts were its huge jaw bones measuring about fifteen feet long. Locals were rumoured to be creeping around, armed with chainsaws, cutting and dissecting the dead creature to remove its giant jaw. Once removed, the jaw was quickly spirited away, apparently on a tractor and trailer, to an unknown location on the other side of the Island. But, just as in Whisky Galore!, when the police and customs officers came from the mainland to confiscate the looted whisky from the islanders, likewise, in this case the police and scientists were quickly on the trail to retrieve the whale bones. The islanders were eventually forced to give up their ill-gotten gains and the jaw bones were left at an agreed location where the police and scientists could find them.

Eventually scientists from Edinburgh University arrived with two big trucks and took the by now, very smelly body of the whale, including the prized jaw bones, back to Edinburgh, where they would eventually reassemble the skeleton for scientific study. However, all was not lost; the scientists cast a life-size model of the jaw bones and presented it to the island. They are now on display on the hill directly above the ferry terminal, and they are one of the first things people see when they arrive on the ferry.

Because the whale had deteriorated somewhat before the press arrived, they were on the lookout for any good photos that had been taken of it earlier – to use in their newspaper coverage of the incident – and that's when I bumped into a couple of reporters in the pub. I said that I had some good photos of the whale and they asked if they could see them, so I went home and got them. We ended up having a good chat and, of course, a drink. They were plying me with wine, after which I agreed to give them the best of the photos. As it turned out, they used one of them for their article in the Daily Mail, showing the whale only hours after it had been beached. They were happy and I was happy that one of my photos had been used, and I thought that would be the end of it. I was wrong.

About a week later I got a phone call from Willy, the photographer I had given my photos to. He said that someone in the pub that night had told him I was a transsexual. Wasn't that nice of them? Anyway, he said that the Mail was interested in my story, and they would like to come back to the island and do an article on me. I told him that I wasn't interested because I was doing well and I didn't want to attract any attention to myself, but his reply was, 'Look, we are coming back to the island anyway and we can easily write about you, with or without your input, so why don't you give us the true version instead of us getting it from others?'

Put like that I really felt that I didn't have any choice but to agree to speak to them. I was accused by some people of selling my story to the press, but it just wasn't like that at all. Another friend of mine, Craig, said that I was crazy to let the press do a story on me. He and his wife Lesley are police officers in Glasgow, but they have a house on Coll, so they are regulars to the island and being pretty good friends of mine, they were naturally concerned for my well-being, as they had had a lot of dealings with newspaper reporters in Glasgow. Craig said that they would destroy me by sensationalizing my story and told me that they wouldn't put over my side of the story as I wanted it, but would make it in to something sleazy, just to make a good story. I told him they had assured me that the story would be entirely based on my input and that they would respect me.

Craig replied, 'That's rubbish – mark my words, they'll destroy you.' By that point everything had been arranged for their visit, so I went ahead anyway.

The following week the Mail sent over a reporter called Don, along with Willy the photographer. They spent nearly two days with me, doing interviews and photo shoots, and I asked them, 'Why me? I'm sure I'm not the most glamorous transsexual in the world.'

They told me that they had come across other transsexuals in their travels but I seemed to be different and special in some way. This made me very happy because, as I've said before, I have always seen myself as being different from other transsexuals. Above all, I wanted to keep my individuality and just be a woman living normally. I had no desire to go to drop-in sessions where transsexuals all met up with each other and didn't mix with anyone else. The whole point for me was – and is – to be a normal female and just fit into society.

Eventually the article was published in the Scottish Daily Mail. It was a page and a half long, accompanied by pictures, and was as promised – a well-balanced and sympathetic, if brief, account of who I was. I became good friends with Willy the photographer and still keep in touch with him on a regular basis to this day. The weekend after the article came out I met Craig and Lesley in the pub. In front of the assembled company, Craig said to me, 'Jules, I'm sorry – the Daily Mail – you were right, I was wrong. They stood by you and told your story sympathetically – well done.' At that we all had a few drinks together, as always.

I had agreed to the Daily Mail story because it was being done anyway, but I was also aware that it would inform the hundreds of people I had known throughout my life about what I was doing. As well as reaching people who knew me well now, but didn't have any idea of my plans, the story would also reach those people I hadn't seen for years. I came to hear plenty of accounts through friends of friends, about people who had seen the article or been told about it, so it really had spread the word very widely.

One of the things that most surprised the reporters when they came to do the article was the fact that nearly everyone just treated me normally. Although only a couple of months had passed since I began living as Julie Clarke, most folk were beginning to accept my decision; they had their own lives to live and my situation was slowly becoming less of an issue. Some people had to try harder than others, but they were getting there, and one or two people had said to me that I was part of the community and I had the right to live in it as I wished. Of course there would be others in the community who would need much more time – months, even years – to get used to it, but in general the attitude of the community towards me was one of acceptance.

The reporters also said that writing about me made a refreshing change; generally they only got to write about transsexuals when they were being discriminated against, or when someone was being violent towards them. I knew what they meant. When I went to the Sandyford for my appointments I would occasionally meet other transsexual people in the waiting room and we would get chatting. All they ever talked about was the abuse they received.

They would ask, 'What about you?' And I would say, 'What about me?'

The response to that would be, 'Don't you get any bother?' And when I said I didn't, they found it hard to believe and wondered how I'd avoided any trouble.

I truly believe that one of the reasons I wasn't getting too much bother at this stage had a lot to do with where I lived, as most of the people who lived in the Isle of Coll were amazingly tolerant and understanding. Also, I was supremely confident and at ease. I tried not to attract attention to myself, especially in the early days, and even now you will hardly ever see me wearing a skirt. To me, you don't have to wear a skirt all the time to be a woman. If I'm on a night out then I will wear a short skirt and high heels, but otherwise I usually wear dressy denims or a trouser suit with a nice top and modest high-heeled boots.

I'm not saying I have never had any issues with anyone since I came out in the open as a transsexual, but any I did have were very brief and low key; just minor things like someone slipping up and referring to me as 'he' instead of 'she', little things like that, which could be infuriating nevertheless. I do have the greatest sympathy for those poor souls who have had to endure endless discrimination and abuse. Living as a transsexual is hard enough without having to put up with all that too.

I still had a way to go, but one thing was for sure: I was on top of the world. I had never in my life felt such elation, such immense optimism, and I could hardly hold back my excitement. Whereas, in the dark old days, I used to hope that I wouldn't wake up in the morning, I now went to sleep with a smile on my face. I was eager for the morning to come, when I would be ready to take on the day ahead with an enthusiasm that I had never dreamed of before.

I still had to keep pushing towards the one thing that would make my life as a woman complete: surgery. There were still dozens of appointments ahead in the build up to what would finally change me for ever. As well as my usual visits to the Sandyford clinic, I would have to get laser treatment for facial hair removal and speech therapy to help change the pitch of my voice. When I'm in the company of people who know me I am a bit lazy and often speak as I used to, but when I'm off the island I speak entirely in my female voice. I really should try harder when I'm at home.

Since all of my appointments and assessments were on the mainland, I was able to get away from Coll for two or three days at a time. Marcia would always come with me and we would treat the trip like a mini holiday, doing what we did best – eating out, going to nice bars and shopping. The appointments were usually in Glasgow and only occasionally in our local mainland town of Oban, but we always booked into the Royal Hotel in Oban if we could, it was our favourite hotel. We were very well known there and I had also stayed there often before I became female.

When I made the change to Julie the entire hotel staff accepted me right away – in fact, they started to treat me as if I was royalty! Without knowing it, the staff at the hotel, from the manager to the housemaids and kitchen and bar staff, actually played a big part in building up my confidence.

At the Royal Hotel the staff, as well as the regular customers, were all getting to know me as Julie. They weren't the only people to say that I was much nicer as a woman than I had been as the man they knew before, and my popularity at the hotel seemed to be mirrored all over the town. I was also becoming well known in the shops and restaurants, and especially to all the taxi drivers – something that had never happened to me before, when I was just that dull little bloke who nobody noticed.

I had turned into a happy, outgoing, optimistic and cheerful middle-aged woman. Men were now holding doors open for me, offering to carry my case up the stairs at the hotel if the lift was full. They would offer me their seat in the bar if it was busy; if I was waiting to cross a busy road they would allow me to cross. It felt good to be a woman and I was becoming more and more confident with every day that passed.

chapter ten

rising acceptance

Living on an island like Coll is definitely more difficult than life is on the mainland. Everyday items are more expensive. There is a two-and-three-quarter-hour ferry journey from Oban to get them here, making everything about ten per cent more expensive due to freight costs. So a lot of people have more than one job to make ends meet. I'm no exception – as well as working at the ferry terminal, which I class as my first job, being a full-time employee of the company, I also run a small building-maintenance business covering quite a wide range of work, from joinery to painting and everything in between.

Another sign that people were accepting me as a woman was that they continued to use my services just as they had before – my workload didn't diminish at all. One of my many clients is Argyll & Bute Council – I do all the maintenance and repairs at the local primary school and at the airport terminal building. As with CalMac, the council had also pledged their full support for me when I was undergoing my sex change, and were happy for me to continue as their local contractor. More importantly, the parents of the children at the school didn't have any issue with me continuing to work there. But the most amazing thing of all was – and still is

– the fact that the children themselves adapted to my change from male to female with complete ease. And now there are a growing number of younger children who have only ever known me as Jules.

As well as working for CalMac and the council, I also do the running maintenance and repairs for Argyll Community Housing Association which owns much of the rented housing on the island. All in all, I am very busy and it is the work ethic that I learned at a young age, as well as my perfectionist nature, that have stood me in good stead.

But it is working at the ferry terminal that means the most to me as it was something I had dreamed of since I first came to the island in the 1960s. Getting my first job there in 1995 was a defining moment for me, another dream come true, and the fact that I'm still doing the job I love, but now as a woman – well, every day I stand on the quay watching the ferry arrive and think just how lucky I am. I mean, how many women get to help dock a six-thousand-tonne ship every day? It is absolutely awesome, and I am passionate about what I do.

I had been living as a woman for about eight months and everything had, so far, been mostly very positive. However, we – meaning everybody concerned with my change – had overlooked one thing, and how we missed it I have no idea. I was still married.

Now that I was a woman, technically I was in a same-sex marriage, and that wasn't even legal at the time – let alone being anything I might still want to be part of, same sex or not. Many calls were made, and emails sent, to rectify this situation as soon as possible and finally, in January 2005 Anne and I were granted a quickie divorce which finally put things right. And more importantly, it broke, once and for all, another link to my male past.

It was now almost a year since I had begun living as a woman and the doctors at the Sandyford Clinic were happy with my progress. In general, people were getting used to me as a woman, although of course there were one or two glitches in the early days. The Coll islanders had worked hard to try and accept me as a woman, and the same must be said for most of my colleagues at CalMac, but one hiccup was due to the unintentional ignorance of a crew member of one of the ships. No one at the company had ever had to deal with a transgender staff member before, so it wasn't really surprising that there was the occasional slip-up. I was off duty for a few days and I'd decided to take the ferry to the mainland for a shopping trip. I needed to go to the ladies' on the ferry, and when I came out of the toilet the chief steward was walking past and said hello. I, of course, greeted him in return and that was that.

When I got back home a few days later, I had a call from our personnel manager at head office. He said that the chief steward had questioned why was I using the ladies' toilet and suggested that in future I should perhaps use the disabled toilets. I pointed out to him that I was legally female; my passport described me as female and I dressed and looked like a female. Furthermore, I said, my place of employment only had a ladies and a gents toilet. Which one did he want me to use and at what point did he want me to start using the ladies? He didn't have an answer right away, but the following morning at nine on the dot he called me to say that the company had taken legal and expert advice because they had never had to deal with anything like this before.

He went on, 'I'm pleased to say we got it wrong. Nothing more will be said about the matter and I apologize on behalf of the company for any distress this episode may have caused you.'

That's how it was left and there have been no further repercussions.

The other glitch at work was much closer to home. This was an issue in my local office and it was disappointing, to say the least. I had always found women sympathetic to my situation, but now I had a female colleague who seemed constantly to be doing me down: referring to me as 'he' and 'him'. I would politely correct her and she would say, 'Sorry, I just forgot', but the same thing happened time and time again. No one else at work seemed to have this problem, so when it kept happening, over and over again, I asked my supervisor if he could have a word with the lady, which he did. This made no difference whatsoever, she continued to get it wrong and it began to look as though her 'forgetfulness' was deliberate. My supervisor passed the issue over to our manager in Oban, who told the woman that she had to comply with the legal requirement to acknowledge me as a female, and if she didn't she would face a disciplinary hearing.

When her 'confusion' about my gender still continued, the woman was given a final warning, at which point she said that it wasn't intentional, she just kept forgetting. She was informed that this was no excuse and she had to make it part of her job to get it right, or face a full disciplinary hearing. At last, this seemed to do the trick, although I was now given the cold shoulder by her. That didn't bother me. I have had to put up with much worse than that over the years and it wasn't long before she left the company anyway. I have had no further problems at work since that time. I am accepted by everyone at work and treated wholeheartedly as the woman that I am.

I was doing very well as Julie, and life was just getting better all the time. Not only had I become supremely confident and optimistic beyond belief, but I was starting to feel a great sense of satisfaction and contentment. I knew that the following year, if I passed all the tests and met the criteria demanded by the NHS, my big day would come and I could have the surgery that would make me female, anatomically and permanently, but for now my sense of achievement was coming from the fact that I seemed to be accepted for who I now was by most people, some of whom were saying that they actually liked me better as a woman than as a man.

At this time there was a steady influx of newcomers to the island, and these people had only ever known me as Julie. Two of these newcomers, a couple called Ian and Terri, would become the best and most sincere friends I have ever had, and when I needed someone by my side they went above and beyond what anyone could expect of even the best of friends. I first met Ian in late 2004. He had retired from a career in business a couple of years earlier and had decided to look for a house in Scotland, which brought him to Coll, where he had come to view a farmhouse that was for sale. He was staying in the Coll Hotel and that's where Marcia and I met him on one of our nights out. We got talking and had a drink together and I offered to help him in any way I could do, telling him that I had a small maintenance business. That first night we met, I just had an intuition that we were going end up being close friends. The next day he went off on the ferry back to the mainland, and a few weeks later we heard that he had bought the farmhouse. The next time I saw him was on the ferry in early February when he brought the first vanload of furniture over for his new house. Marcia and I had been to the mainland on a shopping trip and were returning home. Ian and I recognized each other immediately, but there was a woman with him I didn't know. Marcia and I speculated wildly as to who she was because she wasn't the same woman who had been with him on his previous visit to the island. I didn't get a chance to speak to Ian and his friend since we were nearly home and we were all heading to our cars, ready to disembark from the ferry.

Later that day I went over to Ian's house to offer to help in any way I could, and Ian introduced the mystery woman as his partner, Terri. She seemed to have a twinkle in her eye, and just as when I first met Ian, I knew for certain that we were going to be good friends from that moment.

At first our relationship was purely business. Ian had asked me to help with renovating the house and I agreed to work with them for as long as they wanted, thinking it would be two or three months at best. It actually took two years – although I did have to break off occasionally to attend to some of my regular clients, and of course I also had my full-time job at the ferry terminal.

Ian, Terri and I were spending so much time together that we were becoming ever closer friends. They had totally accepted me as a woman – after all, they had only ever known me as Julie (although, like nearly everybody else, they were soon calling me Jules, which was absolutely fine).

I consider my friends on the basis of their loyalty and commitment to me, and in return they can expect the same from me – unconditional loyalty and uncompromising commitment. The few people over the years who have been unfailingly sincere, honest, truthful and loyal are the ones that I cherish and they know that they can rely on me; Ian and Terri definitely fall into that category. They were part of a small band of six, which also included my ex, Anne, who is the only person on this earth who ever truly understood me and what I was really all about. As I've said before, she seemed to know me better than I knew myself.

Unfortunately the other three in that small group of best friends are no longer around. Sheila Bidwell, my friend from my days in Callander, was the person who first recognized that I was different and confronted me about it over coffee one day. However she then became an enthusiastic supporter and encouraged me to do what I thought was right for me and not to worry about what others might think. She stood by me until she died in 2006. Then there was Sue Clarke in Edinburgh, whose surname I took my own from. She gave me the confidence to get out and about and meet people as Julie; from the day we first met, she was prepared to accept me for what I was – or what I aspired to be, when I was still struggling with that. She encouraged me to climb out of the hiding place I was in at the time and told me to walk tall, be seen and believe in myself. From her I learned that I could do what ever I wanted to do, and every time I get dressed up to go out, I look in the mirror and think, 'Yes, Sue was absolutely right!' Sadly, she died in the late 1990s, but I know she's still watching over me.

Probably the most visible of the true friends I have lost, because she was seen most openly with me and was prepared to take any flak for it, was Marcia. She had been ill for a while, but I was still left with a huge sense of loss and emptiness when she passed away in 2006. I think of Marcia as the bravest of all my friends because she was prepared to be seen with me in the very difficult days, right after I openly became Julie Clarke. She was steadfast in her belief in me and together we presented a united front. The really sad thing is that she isn't around to see Julie as she is today. She would have been so proud of me; she was the one person who mentored me in the art of womanhood. We had endless conversations about how I looked and she was instrumental in teaching me about deportment and how to 'be' in general, especially in the company of men. Marcia played a very large part in my transition and was there for me at a time when I needed all the help and support I could get.

To have lost three such dear and trusted friends has been devastating, but I'm convinced all three are watching over me. They would all, I'm sure, have been delighted with the woman I have become today.

The majority of residents on Coll are now 'incomers' – and I include myself in that category. I only moved here permanently in 1995, although many of the other incomers have been here much longer. Long gone are the days when the island was populated mainly by Collachs. Sadly, the indigenous population is quite literally dying off – even though, having said that, there are now thirty or so children born to islanders and these children are the new generation of Collachs. We incomers, no matter how long we have lived on the island, will always take second place to them, we can never be true Collachs. What we are, though, is an eclectic bunch from an astonishing range of backgrounds and careers. There are managing directors of national companies to former members of the armed forces; doctors, lawyers and accountants, ex members of the police and fire services, former national sports personalities – and even a nuclear physicist, as well as many others. All of us have opted out of a more predictable way of life on the mainland to take our chances on this small island on the edge of the Atlantic

Ocean. It's that diversity of people with their multitude of skills, most of whom have been highly successful in their former careers, that has made the island dynamic, forward-looking, vibrant and prosperous. Many have used their entrepreneurial and business experience to breathe new life into the place.

More recently though, a small minority of those incomers have found that maybe the grass isn't as green on this side of the fence as they might have hoped, and are actively striving to bring in more amenities and services (the 'mainlandization' of Coll), thus destroying the very thing which attracted them to this beautiful and unique island. But don't get me started on that one …

It was by now high summer and the island was bursting at the seams with tourists and all the Coll exiles who come home for their summer breaks. The latter are affectionately known as the summer swallows. They live on the mainland for most of the year and return to their family homes for the summer. Everything happens in summer – the Coll Show, the annual sea-fishing competition, the Coll open golf championships and numerous beach parties, barbecues and dances in the village hall. If the weather is good, it really does feel like you're in paradise.

This summer I was not focused on the fun I could have on the island. I had just received an appointment to meet an independent clinical psychologist in Edinburgh who would decide, once and for all, if I was ready to go forward and make the momentous changes to my body that would be the result of a gender reassignment operation.

My appointment was set for the 10th of August 2005. Despite everything I had been through at the Sandyford – so many consultations and assessments covering a multitude of medical and psychological tests – this appointment was in some ways the most important of my entire life. This man had the power to make or break me. But I was confident that he would agree with all the other experts I had already met, who agreed that I really was a woman trapped in a man's body.

The appointment was at eleven thirty in the morning, and I was there half an hour early. I am never late for anything – indeed, I am meticulous and almost obsessive about punctuality and the need to be where I should be, at the time I should be, to do what is required of me. I was expecting the meeting to be very formal and serious so I was taken completely by surprise when the receptionist called me through to the consultant's room and I was greeted by a cheery-looking little man sitting at the other side of the desk.

He said, 'Hello, Julie. How are you today?'

I replied nervously, 'Very well, thank you. How are you?' Greeting him as I would do anyone immediately took away the tension and got us off on a great footing.

He said right away, 'I see you're from the Isle of Coll – I've been to most of the Scottish Islands but never Coll', and I joked, 'Well, that's terrible!'

He went on to say that he loved travelling on CalMac ferries, and I told him that I worked for CalMac. He began to ask me all about my work and what it was like to be a woman, helping dock those huge ships, as well as what it was like to live in such a beautiful part of the world. This is how the conversation went for half an hour or so, at which point I began to realize that he hadn't asked me any serious questions yet, which worried me. After a little more conversation about nothing in particular, he said, 'Well, Julie, I'm happy to sanction your gender reassignment.'

I was confused, to say the least. 'But you haven't asked me any relevant questions yet!'

His response was, 'I don't have to. For the past forty minutes I have been talking to a woman who clearly loves life and is content with the path she has chosen, or which has been allocated to her by her circumstances. There is no doubt in my mind that you will live successfully as a woman for the rest of your life.' He went on the say he would send his report to the Sandyford Clinic, recommending my full gender reassignment.

After everything I had been through over a period of more than forty years, coming close to the point of total meltdown and descending into oblivion many times, the direction the rest of my life would take was decided in a meeting with a consultant who didn't even ask one question about my troubled and traumatic life! I realize now that he was looking at the person in front of him and not at who, or what, I had been in the past.

chapter eleven

coll's protection

Although the cheery wee man in Edinburgh would recommend that I should have gender reassignment surgery, the doctors and psychologists at the Sandyford Clinic would still have the final say. I was confident that they would all agree, but I still waited nervously for two weeks until I got the official confirmation that they were happy to put me forward for full gender reassignment (also known as sex reassignment surgery).

I can honestly say that I don't remember any other moment in my life when I felt such elation and excitement. I had a real feeling that I was, at last, actually moving forward, and that this particular part of my epic struggle was coming to an end. I also knew that another chapter in my long journey would soon begin and I felt a certain degree of apprehension; I now faced the stark reality that in the next few months I would be undergoing a huge and very complicated operation. Until that time the actual surgery had never even been discussed, but now that I had been judged suitable and the gender reassignment was to go ahead, I was to be observed by a highly specialised surgical team who, for the next few months, would test and monitor me in incredible detail.

After my consultant at the Sandyford had given me the good news, she told me that I had a choice of two surgeons. One was based in Brighton on the south coast of England, and the other was in Edinburgh. We discussed the pros and cons of both. Each surgeon had slightly different ways of doing the surgery in terms of the procedure and the outcome. I won't go into graphic detail – it would be more than you'd want to know, trust me – but in the end I chose the surgeon in Edinburgh. Although I was offered a choice, it was a very easy decision for me to make. This was mostly because the surgeon was a Scotsman and the procedure would be done much closer to home for me. His name was Trevor Crofts and at that time he was a general surgeon, operating in all the main Edinburgh hospitals and also specializing in sex reassignment operations. He was mentored by a surgeon called Jim Dalrymple who oversaw some of Trevor's operations. When I had made this very important decision my consultant at the Sandyford, Dr Susan Carr, contacted Mr Crofts' office and they said they would set an initial appointment for me to meet Mr Crofts to discuss the operation.

Many male-to-female transsexual people take hormones, supposedly to soften and change their body shape and their features. However, I have never been convinced about the benefits of this and Dr Carr was of the same opinion. She was concerned about the possible side effects of these hormone treatments – most notably, there could be problems with liver function after long-term use, as well as serious mood swings and depression, to name but a few. Well, no thank you. I took Dr Carr's expert advice and have never taken any hormones of any sort, and never will; I just don't need them. Having said that, I completely understand other transsexual people may need, or want, to take them. We all do what we think is right for us as individuals and we should respect each other, whatever path we take in life, as long as this doesn't bring harm to others, of course.

Most of the population of Coll had now become quite used to Julie Clarke as she was, despite the huge impact she had had on the island when she emerged as a woman in May 2004. People were aware that in a few months time I would be undergoing a big operation that would change me once again, this time for ever, and people kept asking me when it would be. All I could say was that it would be early the following year, in 2006. I now began to be aware of a subtle change in the way some folk viewed me; people now had to get their heads round me going to the next level which would entail surgery that would change me forever. A few folk said to me at the time, 'Why do you have to have the operation? We have got used to you the way you are.' Some said they were worried I might regret the operation in years to come because they had seen a TV documentary about some male-to-female transsexuals. This documentary had portrayed transsexuals who were desperately unhappy about the gender they had become and who wished they could reverse the surgery, which of course they couldn't. My response was, and still is, that I was different from all the others.

I said, 'I know where I've been, I know where I am now, I know where I'm going and I know that is where I should be. And nothing is going to change that. Otherwise my last forty years of sheer hell would have been all for nothing. There is no way I can or would want to go back, and there is no way I'm staying as I am. Nothing is going to stop me achieving what I have been striving for most of my life.',

Regardless of anything said to my doubters, it was becoming clear that, amongst the islanders, my impending operation had re-ignited all the talk and debate I thought I had left far behind. There were some at least who were genuinely worried for me and didn't want me to do anything that I might regret for the rest of my life.

There is one particular encounter that I will never forget. I was doing some work at the Coll Hotel and was cleaning the window frames at the time. I was making my way down the ladder when I noticed the owner coming round the side of the building. She was holding a tissue to her face and weeping. When I got to the bottom of the ladder I asked her what was wrong, thinking something awful had happened.

She said, 'Jules, do you have to do it?' She told me she had been watching a documentary on sex changes and all the transsexuals in it were messed up and desperately wanted to change back to their original gender if they could. She told me that she didn't want the same thing to happen to me, at which point I became very emotional as well, but I reassured her I was sure that what I was doing was the right thing for me.

'The most surprising discovery for me at this time was to find that those people who knew me well really did care and they genuinely didn't want to see me messing up my life. Knowing that people really were worried and cared about me touched my heart and is something I will never forget as long as I live.

In my own mind I was 100% certain that I would never regret the journey I was about to embark on. In fact, the only regret I had at the time was that I hadn't reached my goal twenty years earlier.

At the same time I understood that I wouldn't have been ready back then. The years of agonising about my body and my feelings of confusion about who I was, had to happen. My body and mind had to go through that long and difficult process of eliminating my male side. I had no doubts whatsoever, though, that I would never, ever, regret where my long journey had at last brought me.

chapter twelve

a stark realization

At last I received a letter detailing my first appointment with my surgeon, Trevor Crofts. Seeing the date of the 15th of November 2005, I felt like the last forty years of my life had been focused on this one day and all I could now think about was what lay ahead. The past was now very much just that, the past; my previous life was gone and I wondered why it had been so difficult to reach this hugely important day. At the same time, I was suddenly struck by the knowledge that very soon I was going to undergo a massive operation. The only other time I was ever in hospital was when I had my tonsils removed at the age of four. I quite naturally became apprehensive until, after a few days I realized that my operation would be easy, compared with what I had already been through in my lifetime.

There were just over three weeks before I met Trevor Crofts and my emotions swung wildly between apprehension and elation for the entire time. I hoped that when I eventually got to meet Mr Crofts he would allay my fears.

Finally the day of my appointment arrived. I was due to meet Mr Crofts at 3.30 in the afternoon, and as ever, I was there one hour early, having stayed in Oban overnight and then travelled down from there on the day. That's one of the drawbacks of living on a remote island – you have to allow three days even for a brief outpatient appointment on the mainland. You travel to the mainland by ferry on the first day, stay in a hotel that night, go to your appointment on day two, have another hotel stay that night and travel back home on the ferry on day three. It's not all bad, though, as the NHS does reimburse the travel and accommodation expenses and sometimes there's time to do some shopping as well!

I arrived in Edinburgh around midday, which gave me time to go for lunch and think about my first meeting with Mr Crofts. I was trying to imagine what he would look like and how the meeting might go. I was sure that it would be extremely formal. When I arrived at reception I must have looked very nervous indeed, because the receptionist said to me, 'Don't worry, Miss Clarke, Trevor will come for you shortly. Just take a seat and relax.'

I could see people going in and out of the consulting rooms and I was trying to work out which one might be him, expecting someone in a white coat to approach me. I was surprised when a very dapper gentleman strode towards me wearing a dark blue sports jacket, a stripy tie, smart grey trousers and highly polished brogues.

He said, 'Hallo, you must be Julie.' When I confirmed that I was, he said, 'I'm Trevor, come on through.' Again this took me totally by surprise. His enthusiasm and confidence almost swept me off my feet, and also gave me a bit of a confidence boost.

When we got into the consulting room the first thing he said was, 'You look great, Julie.'

I replied, 'Thank you, Mr Crofts', to which he said, 'Let's dispense with the formalities – it's Trevor.'

I now felt even more at ease as he asked about my journey down. I explained how getting to Edinburgh and back home again would take three days. He asked me all about where I came from and about my work and after we'd chatted for a few minutes, he said, 'So, you're ready for gender reassignment. I've seen all your medical and psychological records and I agree that you know what you're doing and that you're aware of all the possible implications.' I told him I was, and after some more discussion he said, 'Right, I'm now going to tell you what's involved in the operation and how we carry it out, and then at the end I will ask you if you are still happy with everything. If you are, I'll then ask you to sign a form giving your consent for us to move forward to the next stage, after which we will send you out a date for your surgery.'

Just talking to Trevor made me feel good. His confidence was immense and I knew immediately that I had chosen the right surgeon – and this was even before he began to talk me through the operation. As he did, I was again struck by how informal the conversation was, given its serious nature.

The first thing he said was, 'This is a big and complex operation which takes six to seven hours. In the past people have died during it. However, I have done over forty of them now without any real problems.' I found this last comment quite reassuring, realizing that with any surgery patients have to be informed about what can go wrong.

He then said, 'Right, Julie, I'm now going to talk you through it. I'll draw some diagrams as we go along, so feel free to stop me and ask any questions at any time. It will probably take half an hour or so.' I listened intently to all the graphic details, and after around half an hour, he said, 'Well, Julie, that's roughly it. Are you still happy to go ahead with it?'

Without hesitation I answered, 'Yes, definitely.'

'Are you absolutely sure?'

I replied, 'I've never been more sure about anything in my entire life.'

At this he reassured me, 'That's very good – I'm sure you're doing the right thing.'

What he didn't know at the time was that while he had explained the operation to me in graphic detail, I had just blocked out all the really gory bits, thinking I would just worry even more if I thought about the physical reality of the whole operation. All that remained was for him to examine me and he asked if I wanted a female chaperone present. I said that wouldn't be necessary and soon the consultation was over.

Although Trevor had emphasized to me that this was serious surgery, and that there was certainly some risk involved, I was convinced by his overwhelming confidence and positive attitude that everything would be all right. I left the clinic happy and reassured by Trevor, who said that he was pleased I was now one of his girls – that's how he refers to all of his male-to-female transsexual patients.

In some ways Trevor and his surgical team represented the final chapter in my long journey because they would be the ones to make the necessary physical changes to my body which would finally unite it with my mind.

On the three-hour drive from Edinburgh back to Oban that evening I had time to reflect on my life, and the reality of what was going to happen to me really set in. But I felt more convinced than ever that I was definitely doing the right thing.

*

About three weeks later I received a letter from the Sandyford Clinic telling me my operation had been set for the 18th of February 2006, two days after my fiftieth birthday. Most people's fiftieth birthday is a bit of a milestone, but mine was to be more than that. I was going to take a huge leap and make a momentous change to my body – one which I would never be able to reverse. Personally, I couldn't think of a better fiftieth birthday present. The 18th of February would mark the end of my years of turmoil and herald a whole new life for me.

Although I had all of this going on, I had to keep working and living my life as usual. Work is the key to my success – I'll never be a millionaire, but I've always been quite comfortable, and as an adult I had always owned my own house. In late 2005 I was in a rented cottage, having sold the house I had shared with Anne, but I had a strong desire to have my own house again at some point in the future.

chapter thirteen

the final countdown

I had to focus all my attention on preparing for my impending operation. But first I had to get through what has always been a difficult time for me – Christmas and New Year. For many people who live on their own, no matter what their circumstances, it can be a very lonely time, as I had found out over the Christmas of 2004, my first after emerging as Julie Clarke in the spring of that year. Previously, I had always been invited to spend Christmas Day with a local family, but sadly they had turned their back on me and the invitation just wasn't there any more. However, a lifetime of being shunned and left out had hardened me to this sort of treatment and I tried not to let it bother me too much. But when Christmas Day came that year, the loneliness hit me like a ton of bricks. I didn't even have my old cat Geal for company, she had died earlier in the year. I think this was the point where I realized that the path I was walking was probably going to be a very lonely one.

Realizing that I just didn't have anyone to turn to really did affect me quite badly. I felt like no one cared, if they had then I wouldn't have been on my own. I spent the whole day crying and feeling sorry for myself, although I did cheer up a wee bit when Christmas Top of the Pops came on. The 1973 number one was Slade's Merry Xmas Everybody, which perked me up a bit because its lyrics said it all – my future had only just begun. That apart, Christmas Day 2004 was one of the saddest and loneliest days of my life.

I was still in a very bad state on Boxing Day, but I decided to drive to a beach and go for a walk. Along the way I met two friends, Kip and Carol, who had supported me through my change so far. They asked me if I had had a good Christmas. Well, I completely broke down in front of them and said that I had spent it on my own. They tried to comfort me, saying they had no idea that this had happened, and they promised they would never let it happen again. They have stayed true to their word – I have spent every Christmas with them and their family every year since then. And for that I am truly grateful.

As for New Year, I was extremely apprehensive, as the Scottish custom is, of course, that men and woman shake hands and kiss when they meet each other for the first time in the New Year. I knew for sure that most – though not all – of the local men would try to avoid being in that situation with me and that in turn made it awkward for me as well. I know exactly what they were thinking: they didn't want to have to kiss Jules. To a certain extent that dilemma, for some, still exists to this day although interestingly, none of the men who have come to the island since I became Julie Clarke have a problem with it, even if they have been made aware of my past; they only know me as I am now, and that is as a woman called Julie or Jules.

That's why at the start of 2006 I decided to do something that I have done every New Year since, and that was to have a few days off the island in Oban, where I booked into my regular haunt, the Royal Hotel, where I have many friends, hotel staff and guests.

That first year, there was one couple in particular with whom I got on really well – Ian and Judith. We ended up at the same drinks table one night and immediately hit it off, and we would meet up every day for lunch and then regroup for the festivities at night. We swapped numbers so that we could keep in touch. Ian was really interested in my work with CalMac; he knew most of the ferries and asked me which my favourite was. I told him it was the Lord of the Isles. The following year when we all met again in the hotel bar at New Year, he nodded to his son who left the room and returned a few minutes later clutching something. Ian told me to close my eyes, and when I opened them, he was standing in front of me holding up a painting of the Lord of the Isles which he had done himself! I hugged and kissed him and everyone clapped and cheered, and after that we all had an absolute ball right through the New Year celebrations.

I also spent time with friends and colleagues from the ferry company during my New Year stay in Oban. I had become particularly friendly with some of crew of the ferry Clansman. I have even been invited to their New Year's Day dinner and celebrations on board the ferry. So my New Years in Oban have been very good, and more importantly for me, none of the men there have had any problem about kissing me.

With the festive season over, it was very much back to business: working and gearing up for my impending operation on the 18th of February. I had also been made aware of a building plot that was available on the hill overlooking the village bay. I approached the landowners to say that I was interested if the price was right. The price they were asking was more than I wanted to pay for a site, but I decided to go and look at it anyway. When I got there it turned out to be exactly what I was looking for. The plot had a stunning sea view and was big enough to build two houses on. At the time, though, I only wanted to build a house for myself – it would be my dream home – so I started negotiating with the land owners through our respective lawyers to buy it on condition that I could get planning permission to build a house there. These processes can be painfully slow and it would take around three months to conclude the deal.

My fiftieth birthday on the 16th of February was fast approaching. Terri, who was now my best friend, would be fifty on the 6th of February and there was also a local man whose fiftieth was on the 5th, so we decided to have a joint birthday party on the 5th, as I would be going into hospital just twelve days later.

My life was hectic and I now also had to factor in being off work for at least four months after my big operation. Although CalMac's policy is to give employees full pay when they are off work due to illness, I wasn't sure how they would see my situation because it wasn't as if I was seriously ill and needed the operation. It was my choice to have the surgery and I wouldn't have been surprised if they had said they wouldn't pay me while I was off work this time. But they had supported me ever since I had emerged as Julie Clarke back in 2004 and they stayed true to their word. They agreed to give me full pay while I was off work recovering from my operation. They had proved once again their commitment to me. In fact, they have actually played a big part in my success in the working environment by treating me just like everyone else –

and in return they can be sure that I am totally committed to them since I am loyal and passionate about the company.

My maintenance business was a different matter. I was self-employed and if I didn't work I wouldn't get paid, so I knew I would be taking a bit of a hit there. I also hoped that my regular customers would be prepared to wait until I was fit to work again – which, as it turned out, they all were, even though they had to wait for four months. At the time I was doing a big renovation for Ian and Terri who were, of course, happy to carry on without me while I was recovering from my operation.

With only about a month to go before I went in to hospital, I still didn't know how I was going to get home after my operation. Not a single person had asked me how I was getting there, or more importantly, how I was I going to get back – I would hardly be able to walk, let alone drive. It was disappointing to say the least when none of my long-standing friends offered to bring me home after my operation, but yet again it was the new friends in my life who would be there for me in my time of need. Ian and Terri didn't hesitate to offer to do take me to Edinburgh and back, which was a huge weight off my mind, and they can be sure that if there is ever a time when they need a friend they can count on in a time of need, I will be there for them.

My long-term friends walked away at this time; not because they now didn't like me, but because they had got used to Julie, or Jules. Now that I was going for the operation they were worried it would change my personality and they just didn't want to let the old Julie/Jules go. Thankfully, as far as I am concerned, personality-wise, the operation didn't change me at all.

On the island some people were dragging up old debates about whether it was right that I was having my op on the NHS, and whether something better should be done with its resources. It seemed that everyone was having a last go at me before my dream became a reality, and unfortunately this subject even reared its ugly head at my joint birthday party. The person who brought it up was one of the people I classed as a close friend at the time. That evening she really expressed her feelings to me in a very forthright manner. She had recently watched a documentary on the subject of transgender surgery – and she had also been drinking. Anyway, she said to me in a very loud voice, 'What the fuck are you doing? You will be all fucked up in your head! You're doing something that you can't reverse and you'll have no libido or anything – why can't you just stay as you are?'

I was so upset by her tirade that I can't honestly remember what I said in response, although it was along the lines of, 'It's too late for that now and I could never go back anyway.'

What I do know is that this exchange completely spoiled my birthday party, but that didn't matter to me as my mind wasn't really on it anyway. I know that my friend had to get her feelings off her chest – she must have been bottling everything up for weeks, even months. I didn't hold it against her then and I certainly don't now, and we are still good friends to this day.

The party was over and there were only about ten days to go before I was due to leave the island; this departure on the ferry would be my most emotional one ever from the island. I even had to consider the possibility that if anything went wrong I might not return to Coll alive. This played on my mind quite a bit, but nothing could now stop me going through with my plans. I knew it was my destiny, come what may.

The day before I left Coll for the mainland, I was extremely emotional too. The island held many memories, both good and bad, and I knew that when I returned in about two weeks' time, I would be a very a different person. In an effort to pull myself together I returned the places of my happy childhood holidays on Coll.

Gallanach Beach and the Windy Gap sand dunes were two of my favourite places as a child and as I walked along the beach I felt as if I was right back in those carefree days of the 1960s. That feeling seemed to give me the strength and the overwhelming confidence that I knew I would need to get me through the next two weeks. It was quite windy and sunny that day; the sky was blue, the surf on the sea was huge and the crashing of the waves deafening. I climbed up high onto the sand dunes overlooking the beach and the Atlantic Ocean and felt exhilarated. I felt so alive and I couldn't imagine not being back here again. So I set myself the goal of returning to this wonderful place as soon as I was fit to do so. It was that thought that kept me going throughout my ten challenging days in hospital.

I was due to check in to the Murrayfield Hospital in Edinburgh on Friday the 17th of February, the day before the operation. I had some business to attend to in Oban beforehand and I left the island a few days earlier. Ian and Terri were to join me on the Thursday to take me to Edinburgh the next day.   Having that couple of days in Oban on my own gave me time to reflect on what I had been through to get to where I was now. Although my emotions were running high and nerves were now really kicking in, there was never any doubt in my mind that I would go through with the operation, though I tried not to dwell on the mechanics of it. I decided that I would have the best time I could before going into hospital, where I would in some ways be facing the unknown. I had two days of luxury – nice meals out and good wine – and I even had a two-day fling with a gentleman who was visiting the town. It was definitely a case of being determined to enjoy myself while I could because I just didn't know what lay ahead. Behaving so irresponsibly was completely out of character for me and looking back on those two days, I now realize that the sheer pressure was getting to me and affecting how I was thinking and acting.

Thursday afternoon came and it was time to meet Ian and Terri. While I waited for the ferry to arrive I finally understood that a whole new chapter of my life was about to begin. This journey to Edinburgh represented the end of my old life and although I had no doubt in my mind I was doing the right thing, the reality of the impending operation I was about to undergo had really sunk in and I was feeling very anxious.

We planned to stay somewhere overnight and then drive to Edinburgh the next morning in time for my 10 a.m. check-in. I had booked us in to the Pirnhall Inn, on the outskirts of Stirling, where we arrived about six in the evening. It was only about an hour's drive from the hospital, so we were well placed to get there on time in the morning.

After checking in to the hotel, we went for a meal. I was on strict instructions about what I could eat prior to my operation – I was only allowed certain food like fish and chicken – in truth I had lost my appetite due to my nerves and only picked at my meal. By this point I was also finding it difficult to engage in proper conversation. My mind was running wild and Ian and Terri were well aware that I was not my usual self.

While we were having coffee, Ian became serious and said to me, 'Right, Jules, here we are. You're going in tomorrow . . .' He hesitated for a couple of seconds, which seemed like an age to me and then asked, 'Are you one hundred percent sure this is what you want?'

I looked him straight in the eye and replied without hesitation. 'Yes, I'm sure.'

He said, 'Tell me again, are you quite sure?'

I replied very firmly, 'Yes.', to which he said, 'That's fine – I just had to make sure, because if you weren't able to convince me I would have taken you back home.' At that moment I said to myself, 'These people really do care about me and I must never let them down – no, not in a million years.'

We chatted a bit more, but my emotions were all over the place and we soon retired for the night after agreeing a time to meet for breakfast. As I lay in bed that night, all I could think about was what was going to happen to me on Saturday and why I had to go through all this trauma to find my true self. I thought long and hard about the hand I had been dealt in life and wondered why there was no other way to escape the turmoil that had been going on inside me for so long. I knew that the moment I had waited for all my life had arrived and in around thirty-six hours I would finally be free, come what may. As had been the case for many years, I then cried myself to sleep. This time my tears were not because I was trapped in a never-ending cycle of anguish – I cried out of sheer relief, in the knowledge that my nightmare was almost over.

Needless to say, we got to the hospital half an hour early for my appointment. Having never seen The Murrayfield before, I had been trying to imagine what it would be like, thinking typical hospital building, but as we drove up the drive I got the surprise of my life at the sight of palm trees and manicured lawns! When we entered the foyer, I was surprised again, it resembled a posh hotel rather than a private hospital. But the check-in procedure was much like it was in any other hospital and this was reassuring.

As soon as I had been checked in to my room and settled in, Ian and Terri took their leave, promising to return later that evening. For me it was straight in to pre-op tests and procedures which lasted all day and into the evening. Trevor, my surgeon, visited me a couple of times throughout the day. He was brimming with confidence, which made me feel slightly less apprehensive, though only slightly. I was under no illusions about the enormity of my operation which would take more than six hours to complete.

As the evening wore on, Ian and Terri came back to visit and wished me all the best. They had also intended to come back in the morning to see me before I went to the operating theatre, but they had met Trevor outside and he had told them that wouldn't be possible because there would be too much going on So we said our goodbyes that evening, and I could see that they were unable to hold back their emotions. To me, Ian looked pensive, as if he was blocking any emotion coming through, probably for my sake. But he wasn't able to hold it back for long and I saw him wiping a tear from his eye.

Terri looked serious but confident. She said, 'You'll be fine, Jules.'

This is typical of her − she would want to be strong for me since she knew me well. She knew that if she broke down so would I, although I could see it was a struggle for her too. The truth is that Terri had guided and helped me through many an issue in my private life, but this was clearly the most difficult one so far. I think, though, I did only hold it together at that point because I was in such a daze . . .

I remember thinking that I might never see them again, that they were the best friends I could ever have asked for and that I loved them with all of my heart. Terri later told me that when they left me I looked vacant and lost. I had accepted that whatever would be would be, although I had to consider that I might not make it through the operation.

After Ian and Terri left, I had my final pre-op tests and was visited by the anaesthetist, who explained his role to me. The information was too much for me to take in and I think I said something like, 'Can you simplify that for me please?'

He replied, 'Yes – basically, it's my job to keep you alive.'

My response to that was, 'Oh well, no pressure then,' and he simply replied, 'No worries.'

It was then that it struck me how wonderful all of those people were and what a responsibility they had. They were going to do all of this for me and how grateful I was to them already!

As the anaesthetist left he just said, 'See you in the morning – you'll be fine.' He could tell I was nervous.

Trevor came in for a final visit and brought Jim Dalrymple with him. Jim stood silently at the bottom of my bed, nodding and smiling, and let Trevor do all the talking. After chatting to me Trevor said, 'I can see you're nervous – we'll give you something for that later.' With that he left, saying, he'd see me upstairs in the morning – upstairs being the operating theatre.

A while later the ward sister and a nurse came in and told me they were giving me something to help me relax. I was given the first of two diazepam tablets. I was given a second one at 2 a.m. which put me to sleep. When I got up to go to the toilet at 5 a.m., well, I just didn't have a care in the world. I felt totally relaxed, which I believe was the plan. When the porters and nurses came to take me to theatre at 6.30 a.m., I knew exactly where I was going, but felt no fear whatsoever. I still felt very emotional because I knew this was the final moment of my old life: I had reached the end of this chapter in my incredible journey and I was fully ready to accept what fate had decided for me, one way or the other.

The next few minutes would be the most important and profoundly poignant moments of my entire life. As I lay on the trolley the anaesthetist asked me to turn on my side. I was to be given an epidural which went into the base of my spine. I felt a sharp prick as the needle went in and then my lower back became ice cold. The anaesthetist then told me the next injection would put me to sleep, and again I felt the needle going in, this time into the inside of my arm. I felt the pressure of the fluid entering my vein and as I started to drift away, I vividly remember saying to myself, 'Thank God it's all over. One way or the other, it's all over.'

At that point I didn't care what happened because I just wanted my life, as it had been, to end. If I died on the operating table, well, it was over for sure. And if I did wake up again, my life as I'd known it would still be over. But one way or the other I would be finally free of the turmoil that had characterised my life for so long.

The next thing I knew, someone was shaking me, saying, 'Julie, Julie, come on, wake up, come on, Julie.' I recognized Trevor's voice and knew I had to make an effort, but it felt like I had been in the deepest sleep I had ever had, which it probably was. It took a huge effort for me to open my eyes and drag myself back to consciousness. Everyone around me was saying, 'How are you?' 'Do you have any pain?' and so on – generally assessing me as I came round. I managed to focus on Trevor. It was difficult for me to speak because I was so weak but I managed, 'How did it go?' and he answered confidently, 'Very well indeed, Julie. I'll see you downstairs.'

Once the recovery team were satisfied I was ready to be moved, I was taken back down to my room. My thoughts now were very different to those I had had on the way up in the lift seven hours earlier. I felt an overwhelming sense of relief that I had made it. And more importantly, I was now anatomically a woman. My body and mind were now at one with each other and a psychological weight had been lifted. In other words, the confusion between my body and mind had finally gone.

I knew I still had a challenging time ahead. I would have to stay lying on my back, hooked up to all sorts of equipment for five days, surviving on only water as nothing could be allowed to go in to my bowels. For that time I would be constantly monitored day and night and this would be followed by five more days during which I would be able to start moving around and eat solid food again.

Once I was settled back in my room Trevor came to check me over and reassure me that everything had gone to plan and explain some things to me. Then a nurse came in to say I had visitors. It was Ian and Terri and we had a very emotional reunion. They had a good chat with Trevor and since I was getting tired they left, saying, 'Well done, Jules – we'll see you tomorrow.'

I don't want to go into too much detail about my recovery in hospital; suffice to say that the first five days were some of the most demanding of my life. I had just had one of the biggest and most highly complex operations that anyone could have, and the first five days following it were especially important in terms of recovery and getting back to fitness. Although I had been assured by Trevor I would be as fit and active in six months' time as I had been before the operation, right then that seemed like a very long way off indeed. I was totally encased in a bandage from the waist down and had a catheter inserted into my urethra. I had massage balloons fitted round my legs which operated twenty-four hours a day, constantly squeezing and releasing, to eliminate the chance of blood clots forming in my legs, which could have been fatal. I had to have my temperature and blood pressure taken every hour, although from about midnight till seven in the morning it was only done twice to let me sleep as much as possible. The massage balloons made that very difficult, however.

Throughout those first five days I had several difficult episodes, complications and setbacks all associated with this type of surgery, but surprisingly I had no pain as the epidural was still effective in numbing my entire lower body. I also had morphine on demand by pressing a button by my side. Although the pain management was effective, I had to fight hard to overcome other difficult medical issues, and sometimes that felt like a losing battle. My overriding thought by then was that even if I didn't survive, I'd achieved my goal and was anatomically a woman – that was the most important thing to me. Thankfully, as the days went on my condition began to improve and I got steadily stronger day by day.

Aside from my medical issues there was boredom. Five days

is quite a long time to be lying on your back. I did have a TV and books, but it's very hard to concentrate on anything after such a high dose of anaesthetic, the effects of which can last for a few days. This meant I had to find other things to do to while away the hours. Even just having my door left open was great, as I could watch people walking up and down the corridor, and some would pop in and have a wee chat.

A few cards had arrived in the post and two of them were from old friends on Coll who had turned their back on me when I changed to being Julie in 2004, so that cheered me up a little. As well as Ian and Terri I had a handful of other visitors, all people associated with Coll who lived on the mainland. Sadly, not one member of my family had phoned or visited me which broke my heart at the time. But I knew I had to do what I had always done throughout my life, and that was to get on with things on my own. I had become used to that. The only contact I had was with my mum the day after my surgery when I had phoned her to say that I had got through the operation safely. She was very happy that I was safe, but I realized that the whole concept must have been so hard for her to comprehend. Nevertheless, I was still upset that none of my family had even enquired about me.

Day five after the operation and it was time to have my bandages removed which was quite nerve-racking because the nurses had been discussing this for a couple of days. It was also time to remove the spacer that had been inserted inside my new vagina to stop it closing up after the op. Thankfully this went well and Trevor was able to examine his handiwork, reporting that all was as it should have been at that stage.

I still had a couple of small issues – nothing serious, though it would take many months before the healing process was complete, which was normal after this type of surgery. After six days in bed I was struggling to get back on my feet. When the nurses eased me out of bed, my legs just couldn't take my weight because they had become so weak through my enforced inaction, and it took a couple of days for me to be able to walk. Eventually I was able to move around slowly with care, and although my legs were getting stronger by the day, I was told it would take at least three months before I could walk normally again, due to the slow nature of the healing process in the region of my surgery.

As well as moving around, I was allowed to start eating again and my first meal was consommé. I think it was beef – after being on a diet of water for five days it tasted absolutely amazing. I then gradually moved onto more solid food as my enforced fast came to an end. I have to say, though, that five days on only water was the best detox I have ever had, before or since. Once the effects of the anaesthetic had worn off I was able to focus on little things again, like reading and being able to think clearly and I no longer needed the morphine either, as I was now on very strong painkillers.

As the time to leave hospital came closer I was keen to try and improve my walking. It was getting slightly easier, although it was still quite painstaking. It wasn't the strength of my legs that was the issue – they were quite strong by now. It was more to do with the surgery, which I was told would take many weeks, even months, to heal.

I was also desperate to get outdoors as soon as possible. I had asked the ward sister if I could go outside and she said it would be ok as long as I didn't go too far. I've always been an outdoor person, so my first foray out after nearly ten days indoors was very exciting. The hospital is right next to Edinburgh Zoo and I took myself down to the end of the building. From there I could see small monkeys and lemurs leaping around the trees. When you're bored and not quite yourself it's amazing what makes you happy and this was just another wee thing that helped get me through.

My eighth day in hospital arrived and all was going well. I was hoping to get out on the Tuesday, ten days after I was first admitted, which was the normal time frame for this operation. But this would only happen if Trevor and his staff were happy that I was fit to go, so there was a lot of checking to make sure everything was as it should be at that stage. One of the tests brought up a slight issue, however. My urethra was still swollen and it was decided that I would be kept in until Wednesday morning.

Trevor had been checking me on a daily basis. I was now one of his girls, and he was dedicated to all of us – about forty in all – on whom he had carried out gender reassignment surgery. During one of our many chats he told me that I was unique in having been willing to undergo so much whilst living in such a small and remote community as the Isle of Coll, where the anonymity of the large city just does not exist.

On the Wednesday Trevor finally said that he was satisfied with my progress and I could go home. I phoned Ian and Terri to let them know; they were still on the mainland at their house in Yorkshire, only three hours from Edinburgh. The plan was that they would pick me up that day and we would travel to Oban to catch the ferry to Coll on Thursday, staying in Oban overnight. Unfortunately the ferry was fully booked on the Thursday which meant we couldn't get home until Saturday, when the next ferry would be leaving. Rather than having a three-night stay in a hotel, we decided to go back to their house in Skipton.

Ian and Terri looked after me and kept me as comfortable as they could, but it was a very long three days. All I wanted to do was get home in order to get back into a routine and try to recover as quickly as possible. We finally arrived back on Coll on the Saturday, but the situation had made me aware once again of how hard it can sometimes be living on such a remote island.

chapter fourteen

taking on the world once more

By the time I got home, the effects of the epidural had long worn off and the strong painkillers that I had taken after the morphine had also been stopped, so I was in a lot of pain for the first time since having the operation,. This was to last for six weeks before the pain began to recede.

As has always been the case throughout my life this was another problem I just had to deal with. As usual I had a project on the go and it helped to keep my mind off the pain. My plan to buy a building plot on the island and build a new house was at last making some headway.

I couldn't shake my anxiety about how people might view me now that I'd had the operation and was now anatomically a woman. The reaction I was getting from them wasn't the reaction I'd been expecting. Most people I met on my short walks to the shops or along the sea front just said, 'Hi Jules, how are you doing?' and not much more. Some would not even broach the subject because they didn't know what to say. The other thing that bothered me was that no one came to visit me and I felt a bit disappointed and hurt at the time, thinking no one was interested or cared.

A couple of folk did explain to me later that they didn't come round because they didn't want to put themselves, or me, in an awkward situation, which was fair enough, I suppose. And those who had been critical about me getting the operation on the NHS didn't want to go on about it any more. What was done was done. Over time, most folk came to accept the fact that Jules was now anatomically a woman and they became increasingly courteous to me once that they got used to the 'new Jules'.Eventually I started to get out a bit more and was tentatively driving again, with extreme care (and against the advice Trevor had given me), so that I could visit Ian and Terri who lived about two miles away. Apart from them and my next-door neighbours, Pauline and Julian, who brought me meals when I first came home, I didn't have much contact with anyone apart from the doctor, of course. None of my work colleagues came to visit and I was becoming increasingly lonely. This was nothing new. I've known loneliness for most of my life and to a certain degree, I still do to this day.

Six weeks after my operation it was time to go back to Trevor in Edinburgh for my check-up. Although I had been in touch with him on the phone about the pain, which by this time had almost gone, I was really excited about seeing him again and I was keen to let him have a look at his handiwork. I also wanted to tell him how it was changing my life already, as well as thank him properly.

After the full check-up, Trevor was happy to sign me off for good, which surprised me, but he said there was no need for any further check-ups as my healing and recovery were good.

His final advice to me was, 'Go and enjoy life as a woman. You risked everything to get where you are now. Life is precious, live it to the full.' We then said our goodbyes and he wished me the very best of luck for the future. By the time I got out to the car park I had tears in my eyes. I still think of Trevor fondly and we swap emails occasionally. I have invited him and his wife to come to Coll for a wee break, which they say they will get round to one year.

It was now April 2006 and I was starting to do a little light work in my maintenance business which was helping me to get as fit as I could in preparation for going back to work at the ferry terminal – something I was desperate to do as soon as possible. I would need to be 100% fit before going back there, though, as you need a bit of strength when hauling the ships' ropes. The company doctors would have the final say as to when I could go back.

My time off work did allow me to concentrate on concluding the deal to buy the building plot and plan my new house with my builder. With the conclusion of the land deal getting closer, I was now starting to think about the financial aspect and that was another reason I wanted to get back to work. Although I was on full wages from CalMac for the whole time that I was off work I was self-employed in my maintenance work, so if I didn't work I didn't get paid. I had over £50,000 in the bank left over from the sale of my boat charter business, this was only enough to buy the land and pay for the planning permission and the solicitor's fee. On top of that, I still had to finance and build the house and the cost of that would be close to £100,000.

I was so desperate to get back to work that there was a point in mid-May when I thought I had taken on too much. Dealing with my house plans and the aftermath of my operation became very stressful. I had to learn very quickly to pace myself and allow a bit more time for my full recovery from what had been a major operation.

At long last the legal wrangling between our solicitors was over and I was able to give my builders the go-ahead to start building the house. I did the first piece of groundwork myself by symbolically laying a culvert pipe across what would, in a few months, be the entrance to my driveway.

Eventually the time came when all the doctors concerned agreed that I was fit to go back to work at the ferry terminal. I would start back on the 15th of June 2006, after being off work for four months. The Julie Clarke who was returning to work would be a very different person to the one who had gone off on the 15th of February. Back then, I knew the mission I was going on would be life changing and I was in tears and full of emotion, as well as apprehension, on my final day before I went off for my operation. However, when I returned to work on the 15th of June I was full of confidence, optimistic and on top of the world. I was ready to take on that world once more, a world that for so long had conspired against me. Although I had been living successfully as Julie Clarke for the last two years, the day I went back to work at the ferry terminal to the job I loved, in some ways heralded the beginning of my new life.

My body and mind were now living as one and all my confusion and disillusion had gone. I now went to bed at night with a huge smile on my face and when I woke up in the morning I was eager to get out there and take on anything life threw at me. I now only allowed positive thoughts to enter my mind and wouldn't accept anything negative or dark in my world. I'd had half a century of that and now I just don't do darkness.

Being back at work really was the best thing for me in many ways. I was meeting people again, locals and visitors alike, some I hadn't seen since before my operation. My job is as high profile as it gets on the island in terms of meeting people. In a way I have contact with almost everyone who enters or leaves the island. I have to collect the tickets of those boarding the ferry and I also greet those disembarking. In fact, because of my position at the mooring station, where I catch and let go the ships' ropes, I am the first person people see when they arrive at the island and the last person they see when they leave. I am sure there is no one else on the island who has had their photo taken more than me as cameras are always flashing from the decks of the ferries as they arrive in the harbour or leave. Occasionally someone will send me the photos. I even once had one that just said 'Julie Clarke, Isle of Coll'. I presume these total strangers got my name from the badge on my uniform.

I was now overseeing the building of my new house and the most stressful part was keeping the bank manager happy. The build started to go over budget which was probably my own fault. I was back working by then, but the after effects of the operation were still affecting me and I still wasn't as sharp as I should have been. So, because of the financial straits I was in, I took on quite a large bridging loan until the build was completed and the pressure was on to work hard to pay for it. All I now seemed to do was work, work, work, and I simply didn't have time to enjoy my new-found – and hard-won – womanhood, but I was determined to get everything done so that I could live my life as I intended.

By the end of July the new house was more or less finished and finally, on the 25th of July 2006, I moved into my dream home.

The house is situated on a hill overlooking the estuary and village bay, with the open sea beyond, and was more special to me than any other house I had ever owned. It was the culmination of my life's work and I put everything I had into it. What made it so special was that it was Julie Clarke's house, mine alone, and I'm so proud of that. I achieved that goal in the same year as I achieved my gender reassignment. Yes, 2006 had been a tumultuous year so far, but for the first time in my entire life I was truly content. So I had no trouble when it came to naming the new house – it is called Ancaster Cottage, named after the farmhouse where I was born in Callander, the place where I had a happy and carefree childhood before my gender confusion set in. I still had a long way to go in terms of making my house absolutely perfect and I was also aware that I had even further to go in terms of perfecting Julie Clarke.

I had been fairly comfortable financially for most of my adult life, but since I built the new house this changed. I had completely overstretched myself, to the point where it was touch and go every month. I had to channel everything into making sure the mortgage was paid before anything else and there was one point at the end of the year when I only had £4.50 left in my bank accounts. But I was damned sure I wasn't going to lose my house so I had to come up with a plan. In some ways it was obvious, the solution was right in front of me when I looked out of the window, but I just didn't notice it because I was so busy working and worrying about my situation.

After I had built my house I still had a huge chunk of land lying idle and I began to realize it was far too big for me to ever turn in to a garden. That's when I came up with the idea of getting planning permission for another house, with the intention of selling it, in the hope that this would get me out of the financial hole I now found myself in.

After much negotiation with the council planning department, I finally got planning permission for a second house. I immediately divided up my land, which still left me with a large garden, and put the new building plot up for sale. But it was now early 2007 and the credit crunch was beginning to bite. The property markets had collapsed and no one was buying, so my financial difficulties continued.   With no money to spare this wasn't the greatest of times for me although I knew that the building plot would sell eventually – I just had no way of knowing when. I knew I would have to be patient and keep working just to stay afloat. I wasn't able to get out much and I certainly couldn't afford to go to the mainland, let alone have a holiday. Much as I longed to I still couldn't get out and show Julie Clarke off to the world. Despite this, I was still totally content in myself, knowing that some day my fortunes would change. That said, loneliness has been a constant feature of my life, right through to the present day. Until a person has experienced being utterly alone, with no one to turn to, no one to share hopes and dreams with, they can have no idea how truly isolating loneliness is, and for me it has been profound at times. Even if there are lots of folk around it can still affect you. Always having had to hide my inner feelings at all cost meant that I had learned very early on to withdraw into myself. Even in the company of others I could never share my thoughts with anyone; the only place I could live out my desired role as a female was behind closed doors, alone. And it seemed like the loneliest place on earth. After my secret came out in the 1980s, the way I was often treated by others meant that even in a crowd I was often left standing on my own, shunned by almost everyone.

By the spring of 2007 I had a come a long way since those days, but even so, loneliness was still there. Yes, I do have this high-profile job where I see hundreds of people some days and I have a lot of interaction with mates at work and with the travelling public, but at the end of the day it's back home to my own space and that can become very lonely indeed. I'm sure this doesn't apply only to the likes of me; loneliness affects people from all walks of life who find themselves on their own, for whatever reason. But I got to a point where I decided I needed some kind of companionship since I didn't have a boyfriend or partner. I did have my dream house, but it wasn't complete. I had now been living there for a year and I knew there was something missing, something that I always had in my life in the past. That missing link was a cat.

My beloved cat, Geal, had died in 2005 at the ripe old age of seventeen and I now felt I was ready to welcome a new cat into my life. So the search was on. I wasn't keen on a Coll cat. I felt that too many of the island cats were closely related and I thought I would try and find one on the mainland. Life is full of coincidences though, and one day while I was checking in passengers going to the neighbouring island of Tiree, I happened to meet the Tiree vet, who had been on one of his regular working visits to Coll. I asked him if he ever came across any kittens on his travels and he told me that he did, his neighbours on Tiree often had kittens on their farm. I asked him if he could watch out for one for me.

A few weeks later I got a call from him, asking if I still wanted a kitten as his neighbours had a five-week-old litter. He said he was coming to Coll in about a week and could bring one over if I was interested. I excitedly said yes please and he said he would let me know when he was coming over. He phoned a couple of days later to say that he would be over on the first Monday of

July – only about four days away. The ferry running that day was the Lord of the Isles, often shortened to Lotti. I was really excited and just couldn't wait to meet my new companion. I had to be patient, the vet said he would leave the kitten in our office for me and I wouldn't see her until I finished casting off the ferry. As it turned out my work mates all got to see her before I did. When I finally came into the office I was united with my new companion, a beautiful and tiny six-week-old kitten. One of my colleagues suggested that I called the kitten Lord of the Isles, knowing that was my favourite ferry, but I said, 'No, it's a female kitten, so it will have to be Lotti,' – and that's how she got her name.

chapter fifteen

finally being accepted

Due to my shortage of money at the time, my house wasn't quite as complete as I would have liked it, although it was still fairly impressive. The one thing I did have right was the colour scheme, featuring bright yellows and light pastels. This totally reflected my optimism and my positive outlook on life and gave a bright, light and positive feel to the whole house.

I had now been in the house for a year and I also had my kitten, so I felt it was time to have a low-key house warming. I quickly decided on a date – the 20th of July, only about ten days away – and I invited anyone I met and told them to pass the word around.

A huge step forward for me was that my brother George and his partner Joan had recently contacted me to say they wanted to come to Coll to visit me. This was the first time that any of my family, apart from my mum, had made contact with me since I had emerged as Julie four years earlier. They would be there at the party and since it was the first time Joan had met me, she has only ever known me as Julie. We hit it off right away and have been close friends ever since.

Although I had come a very long way since Julie's emergence

in 2004 and I really did feel completely accepted by most people on the island, I was still a little nervous about how many people would come to my house-warming party. I just had no idea. On the night, I was taken completely by surprise when more than fifty people came bearing cards, gifts and best wishes. More importantly, along with my loyal and closest friends, even those who had turned their backs on me and those who couldn't, wouldn't or didn't want to face me in the early days were mostly all there too. But most importantly, as I've said, my brother and his partner were there and that was great because it let them see that I had huge support on the island. And it also let my friends and acquaintances on Coll see that I had some support from some of my family at least.

The success of my party provided a tremendous boost to my already bright outlook on life and another sign that I had achieved a high level of acceptance came shortly after, from work colleagues at the Oban ferry terminal on the mainland.

I had a few days off work and had gone to Oban on one of my regular shopping trips. I was due to travel back home on the ferry early the next morning and wanted to leave my car at the terminal overnight. The ferry-docking and car-park staff, who all happened to be male that day, were on their break, so I had to go into their mess room to ask where I could leave my car for the night. The staff room is a typical male environment and I didn't want to just walk in, so I knocked, tentatively eased the door open and said, 'Hi boys, can I come in?'

As I popped my head round the door, the reception I received was amazing –all I could hear was, 'Jules! Come on in, doll!' Another one said, 'How's it going, pet?' Someone else said, 'How's your darts skills? What's it to be, tea or coffee?' And that's how it went. Remarkably, this was a huge turnaround from the early days soon after I had emerged as Julie, when those same workmates had laughed and joked about me. Being treated entirely naturally like this really did confirm to me that my life had changed beyond all recognition. I was fully accepted as Julie now.

Money was still as tight as ever, and worryingly, I was getting virtually no interest in my building plot due to the ongoing credit crunch. It had been almost a year since I put it on the market and only two people had shown an interest in it, but neither had taken it forward. I didn't want to lower the price too much as I was only going to get one crack at this and I wanted it to make a difference to my life. I had to hold out for a good price even if that meant waiting another year. The summer tourist season would soon be here again and I was hoping a rich holidaymaker would come along and snap it up. Unfortunately, though, as the summer went on it became clear that this just wasn't going to happen and I became resigned to the prospect of another lean winter with no money. But, as often happens in life, something comes along just when you're not expecting it.

My lucky break was to come from the most unlikely person – my ex, Anne, from my life before Julie. After a spell in Callander she had moved back to Coll permanently and she approached me one day and said, 'Jules, did the folk in the big camper van come and see you yet?'

I asked her who she meant and she told me she had got talking to a couple in the cafe the day before who had said they would love to live on Coll, at which point she had told them there was a building plot for sale just up the hill and given them my phone number. Although they had not phoned me yet, this news got me very excited, and I had to find out if they were really interested as I was getting desperate. So I drove around to look for their big camper van and discovered it outside the Island Cafe again. I decided to go in and introduce myself to them – if you don't ask you don't get, after all. Well, it couldn't have gone better, they were very friendly and genuinely interested in the land, and we arranged they would come up later to have a look at it and a chat.

When I came out of the cafe I went straight up to Anne's house to thank her. 'If they buy it it's worth a couple of hundred quid to you,' I promised her, to which she said, 'Brilliant – I'll hold you to that, Jules.' Despite our complicated past together, we still behave in a very civil way towards each other.

After the success of my brother's visit with his partner the previous year, I was pleasantly surprised to get another phone call in 2008, this time from my older sister Rosie. We had a very long talk, where we both apologized to each other for not keeping in touch. It was true that I hadn't contacted her either and I suppose I just assumed that she wouldn't want to know me. I had got that wrong to a certain extent, and it was great to get to know my big sister again. That summer, she and her husband Mike and his sister came over for a holiday, and my sister Rosie got to know her new sister Julie.

I have also kept in contact with Mum and Dad by phone, ever since my operation. Usually only about every six weeks or so, but they are quite happy and have come to terms with everything as best they can. They know it's what I had to do and they would rather that I was happy than not. So even if it's been a bit reluctantly, at least they have accepted me as I am now. I understand that not everyone found it easy to readily accept my decision to become a woman; it's a difficult concept to get your head around at the best of times

There is only one member of my family with whom I have had no contact for at least ten years, and that is my other sister. From what I can gather she has no interest in talking to me, so I've just left it at that.

The prospect of my selling the building plot was looking good. The couple with the big camper van seemed very keen on it and we had been in constant contact with each other since August. We were close to agreeing a price for the plot and in early November it was settled and I received a substantial cheque that would quite literally change my life.

I was now able to pay off a huge chunk of my mortgage and keep a decent lump sum back for a rainy day. I could also have a few luxuries for the first time in over two years and get to the mainland, where I hadn't been for nine months, for some much-needed retail therapy – and, more importantly, an Indian meal. Nine months is a long time to go without a proper curry . . .

There was also one other very important thing I had to do as soon as possible. As soon as I could, I went to Anne's with the two hundred quid I had promised her, and we sat and had a cup of tea and a good laugh about it. That's something I would never have dreamed could have happened, a few years previously, when we were in the middle of our break up.

Financially I was back on my feet again and this meant that I was now able to go on holiday again. The problem was that I couldn't think of anywhere I would feel comfortable going as a single woman. In the end, some business clients from my maintenance work came to the rescue. John and Caroline own a large house on the island with their extended family. I had been doing work for them for at least ten years and we had become very good friends. They had seen me go through my whole transition from male to female and supported me all the way, and I have stayed loyal to them by continuing to look after their property on the island. Their main home is in North Central London, in the beautiful area of Primrose Hill – between Camden Town and Regent's Park – a quiet oasis in a bustling city, with easy access to the whole of London. They invited me to go and stay with them in London any time I wanted. It seemed like a great idea, so I went for my first holiday there in October 2009 and I soon fell in love with it. There is so much to do, especially for someone on their own.

Although John and Caroline always manage to spend some time with me, going out for meals and to the theatre and the like, I enjoy going out and about doing the London things on my own. I just love central London; the restaurants, the theatres, the museums, Covent Garden, the river trips, the wine bars, the live music venues –the list goes on and on, and to me it's the most exciting place I've ever been. Since 2009 I've visited London a few times every year and I love it more each time. I can do all the things I've been missing out on by living on the island.

After I've been in London I really find it hard to come back to Coll knowing that it's back to work and back to business as usual with no time to enjoy my womanhood, doing all the nice things like dressing up and, very importantly, wearing high-heeled boots – it's usually work boots or wellies when I'm back on Coll. I do live a very fulfilling life on the island, but the difficult part is the contrast between there and the mainland. Most of my time is spent here on Coll, due to my hectic work schedule, but going to London – or anywhere on the mainland really – and being able to show Julie Clarke off to the world is becoming increasingly important to me., It may be that the time will come when I decide to leave the island in order to make the very most of my hard-earned womanhood.

For now though, Coll remains my home – after all, it's where I live with my best friend and companion, my little cat Lotti. She's my family and she gives me unconditional love which I return in full. Without her my loneliness would be even more profound than it is, even with my many friends and acquaintances.

Another positive that began to creep back into my life – a throwback to my past and even more proof that I was fully accepted as Julie – was that I was once again in demand for my percussion skills, now as a woman. It was common knowledge that I was an experienced drummer and some local musicians and bands began to ask me if I wanted to join their outfits, or if not, whether I would at least play drums with them on occasion. Although I didn't want to commit to anything long term as I just couldn't afford the time, I said I would be happy to stand in or do one-off gigs now and then as long as people were happy for me to just turn up on the night.

In many ways I was gradually getting back to doing a lot of the things I had done in the past, but I was now doing them as a woman. And that was how people now saw me – as a woman – with many commenting that I was a much better person for it. They were now saying that they realized I had done the right thing with my life and praising me for my courage. To hear people saying this was very heartening indeed, and presumably they were saying the same to each other too. This positive and supportive vibe wasn't restricted to the island, but was coming from people from my distant past on the mainland too.

On one occasion in particular, I was on the ferry travelling to Oban on one of my shopping trips when I was approached by a man and his friend who had been on holiday on the island. It was his second time there in fact, as he had also been there in 2009. He recognized me and said that he was a friend of an old friend of mine called Trish from back home in Callander. We talked at length (the ferry takes two and three quarter hours to get to Oban). He said that Trish was asking after me, that she was happy with the path I had chosen in life and that she respected me for that. He then said that although he had only known me for two years, he was also respectful of the path I had taken and we sat and chatted for the rest of the journey before swapping email addresses and going our separate ways when we got to Oban.

This encounter showed me yet again how wide-ranging acceptance was now, for me and what I had done, and it came from those who had known me for most of my life as well as from those who had more recently become acquainted with me. This was more proof to me that, at last, society was changing in terms of accepting those of us who had taken an alternative path in life. There are still isolated occasions when this acceptance takes a couple of steps backwards, but I am pleased to say that this is diminishing with time.

One thing that hasn't come into my life yet is male companionship of a romantic nature. I do have male friends and acquaintances, but that's as far as it goes. A romantic relationship is something that I desire, but I'm not going searching for it as I believe that what's for you won't go by you and if you think about something constantly it never seems to happen. My Mr Right will just come out of the blue some day, through a chance meeting or situation when I'm not expecting it – that is what I firmly believe.

I have had my moments, but these were only brief encounters – I suppose you could call them flings. Two were with men who hadn't known me as a man and two were with men who had known me before my change, which again proves a very high level of acceptance. Those men just saw me as the woman I am now and not as who I was before.

I also miss having a family round about me. I look on enviously when I see family groups enjoying their time together and it makes me sad when I think of myself on my own and my profound loneliness kicks in once more. But for now I just have to accept that that's the way life is and it's the price I've had to pay for something I never had any control over, though I find it painful and hard to take at times.

I do have many friends and acquaintances, but I can narrow down my true friends to only two. Ian and Terri have been with me all the way since they came into my life in 2004, at arguably my most difficult time. They are loyal, trustworthy and above all sincere and genuine – as well as being good company and great fun to be with. I also have my beautiful house on this beautiful island, and most of all I have my best friend and companion, my little cat Lotti. She's all I have in the world and I love her with all my heart.

My long and arduous journey has taken its toll and I came close to total destruction on quite a few occasions. I was bullied by my schoolmates and persecuted by my teachers because they didn't understand me. I was given no help or encouragement in anything I did and wasn't ever given the chance to show what I could do, which forced me to just go it alone. I was discriminated against at work by those who should have known better in the workplace, and socially I was shunned by those who couldn't or wouldn't accept me for what I was.

So, when I look at myself here and now in 2014, I realize that for most of my life I couldn't have imagined in my wildest dreams that I would be where I am now, having achieved almost total acceptance and living successfully as a woman in every aspect of my life.

The odd person still forgets and says 'he' instead of 'she' when referring to me, but they are few and far between and it's always someone who knew me in the past. When this happens, I just politely correct them and they are usually apologetic. And yes, I do feel that I have to correct them. I have not battled with prejudice and nastiness and my own utter confusion over the years just to let a slip of the tongue go, even if that does sound a wee bit bitchy. Physically becoming a woman was momentous for me. It's who I am and is hugely important to me. But little mistakes like that really aren't a problem and don't take away any of the great elation that I feel on a daily basis.

When I finally emerged as Julie Clarke in May of 2004 the people of the Isle of Coll had the power to make or break me. As far as I know only two people on the island had ever known another transgender person besides me, and the fact that the community was able to embrace me to the extent they did is absolutely incredible.

I will be forever grateful to them and thank them from the bottom of my heart for giving me my life back. I came to Coll hoping to escape from Julie, but ironically Coll was the catalyst that made becoming Julie a certainty.

When I was recovering from my gender reassignment surgery back in 2006, I decided that it didn't matter what happened from then on. I had achieved my objective and if I was to die at that point, I knew I had made it. I had become my true female self and had followed my heart, my mind and my body to become the woman I was destined to be. And nothing can ever take that away.

I set out to write this book for no other reason than to simply recount the trials and tribulations of going through life as a transsexual or transgender person. I didn't write this account of my life in any way to try and get sympathy, or to try and convince people that they should accept transgender people from now on. It is for each individual to make their own mind up on such matters, while drawing on information available to them and on their own experiences. However, as I progressed with my manuscript I began to realize that this book could help give some people a better understanding of just what transsexual people have to go through, to become their true selves, and that I could show that it's not a lifestyle choice, or brought about by some kind of sexual desire, but is something that we are born with and have no control over. And if I do help some people to see transsexuals in a more sympathetic light, well, that really would be a bonus, and hopefully will make some other transsexuals' lives a little easier as a result.

For other transsexuals, particularly those who are still in the early days of their transition, whether this be male to female or female to male, I hope that my story will go some way to giving you the courage to move forward and have faith in yourself and follow your heart and mind. Only when you have eliminated all the other possibilities can you take that momentous step, because you only get one chance and you have to be sure this way is the way for you. It will be a long and lonely path, but if it's meant to be you will get there. However, you will need help, and if you're as lucky as I was, there will be those who will support you and be there for you when you really need them. You will also need sheer determination and above all, belief in yourself. If you have all of those things you can do it – I am living proof of that.

The great sense of achievement and absolute contentment I feel is very real, but there is one thing that continues to bother me, even though it's ridiculous, really. I've always had a wild imagination and my worst nightmare is waking up one morning and realizing that the last eight years have just been a dream and I'm still my old self: that little bloke that nobody noticed or liked. That very thought makes my blood run cold.